The Case
of the
Phantom Friend

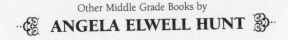
ii

NICKI HOLLAND MYSTERIES

The Case
of the
Phantom Friend

Angela Elwell Hunt

Tommy nelson
for tweens and teens

A Division of Thomas Nelson Publishers
Since 1798

www.thomasnelson.com

Published in Nashville, Tennessee, by Tommy Nelson®, a Division of
Thomas Nelson, Inc. Visit us on the Web at www.tommynelson.com.

Scripture quotations are from the *International Children's Bible®*, *New Century
Version®*, copyright © 1986, 1988, 1999 by Tommy Nelson®, a Division of
Thomas Nelson, Inc.

Tommy Nelson® books may be purchased in bulk for educational, business,
fund-raising, or sales promotional use. For information, please e-mail
SpecialMarkets@ThomasNelson.com.

This is a work of fiction. Names, characters, places, and incidents either are
the product of the author's imagination or are used fictitiously.

Interior: Jennifer Ross / MJ Ross Design

ISBN 1-4003-0764-3
Printed in the United States of America
05 06 07 08 09 WRZ 9 8 7 6 5 4 3 2 1

One

Nicki Holland leaned forward on her bicycle and pedaled faster to catch up with her friends Christine Kelshaw and Laura Cushman. A cool breeze caught her by surprise. About time autumn came to Florida! Though it was mid-November and snow blanketed half the country, Florida had remained warm and sunny.

"Hey, feel that breeze?" she called as she pulled up alongside her friends. "Feels like cooler weather is almost here."

"Thank goodness." Christine let go of her handlebars and sat up straight. Her long red hair sailed behind her in the wind. "My mother's been Christmas shopping for two months and I can't even get in the mood for Thanksgiving. What do I have to be thankful for—my latest batch of freckles?"

Laura shook her head. "You're crazy. You've got a lot going for you. Why, I'd think it was neat to have all your brothers and sisters. My Christmas will be just me, my mom, and my sister, who'll be home from boarding school. Mom's talking about going to Switzerland for the holidays because she doesn't want to be home . . ." She looked down at her tennis shoes and let her bike coast. "Well, the holidays haven't been the same since my dad died."

Nicki glanced over at her friend. "If you aren't in Switzerland or London or wherever, you've welcome to come to my house if you get lonely," she said, trying to lighten the mood. "Now—I'll race you two to Meredith's!"

The girls sprinted on their bikes toward the apartment complex where Meredith Dixon spent weekends with her dad. Laura's lightweight racing bike could have won the race if anyone else had been on it, but Laura was a little wobbly. Her chauffeur usually drove her anywhere she wanted to go.

Nicki and Christine were sprinting with all their might when suddenly a metallic pop broke the steady whir of their bikes. Christine squealed. "Ohmigoodness! My chain broke!"

Nicki stopped pedaling and looked at her friend. "Is that bad?"

"I don't have any brakes!"

In Christine's family almost everything was common property, and her bike had logged the miles of four kids. The weary bicycle chain had given up and was now dragging in the dust. Christine was headed for the intersection where Palm Avenue dead-ended at River Road. If she didn't stop, she'd go over the bank and land in the river!

Christine buzzed past the apartment complex. She was almost to the intersection when Nicki yelled, "Pull off the road! Head into those bushes!"

Terror-stricken, Laura stopped and straddled her bike in the middle of the pavement, her mouth open in a long, never-ending scream. Nicki thought Christine had frozen in fear, but at the last minute she jerked the bike over the curb and into a hedge. The bike stopped, but Christine didn't. She flew over the handlebars and the tall hedge in a somersault. Nicki and Laura watched in amazement.

Laura stopped screaming as suddenly as if someone had flipped a switch. She stood silent for a moment, then looked at Nicki. "Do you think she's dead?"

Nicki rode over to the sidewalk, dropped her bike, and pulled Christine's out of the hedge. "Chris," she called through the greenery, "are you okay in there?"

A weak gasp was all she heard in reply.

Nicki ran to the end of the street and darted through a narrow opening in the hedge. Christine had landed in the yard of a beautiful old Victorian house, probably one of the oldest in town, but Nicki didn't pause to look around. She ran toward her friend, who was lying on her back in a bed of shredded mulch.

Behind her, a screen door slammed and a delicate voice called, "Young lady, is she all right?"

Nicki knelt by Chris's side and looked at her friend's pale face. "Christine?" She tapped her cheek. "Can you hear me?"

Chris opened her eyes and groaned. "I'm going to kill my brother for this," she muttered, her teeth clenched. "He was supposed to put a new chain on that bike."

"Did you break anything?" Nicki grabbed Christine's hands and pulled her up. "Are you sure you're okay?"

"I'm fine. Just had the wind knocked out of me." Christine brushed mulch off her jeans and shirt. "Good thing this flower bed is soft."

"Young lady"—the voice from the porch sounded firmer this time—"are you sure you're all right?"

Nicki remembered her manners and turned to see who had come out of the house. A silver-haired woman stood there, as slender and pretty as the wooden trim on her house. In her arms she held a brown Pekingese whose button eyes were alert.

"Yes, ma'am, she's fine," Nicki answered. "It's a good thing you had mulch in that flower bed instead of rose bushes."

Christine wiped a smudge of dirt from her nose, then grinned at the woman. "I'm sorry I flew through your hedge. Hope I didn't break anything."

"You couldn't hurt that old hedge." The woman smiled in relief. "Would you girls like to come in and rest a bit? You shouldn't take right off after a fall like that."

Nicki was about to answer, but at that moment Laura rushed over to the gate, her bike propped on one hip and Nicki's on the other. "Chris," she called, "should I call Mother's driver to come pick us up?"

Laura must have noticed the woman on the porch, because she blushed. "I'm sorry, I didn't mean to interrupt. I'm Laura Cushman, and these are my friends, Nicki Holland and Christine Kelshaw."

Nicki grinned. She could always count on Laura to remember her manners in a time of crisis.

The lady smiled. "I'm Lela Greaves," she said, "and this"—she held up her tiny dog—"is Buttons. We insist that you all come in for some lemonade and a cookie or two. Once you've taken a fall like that, you've no business just heading up and away."

The girls looked at each other. "Meredith is expecting us," Laura reminded them, "and Kim will be meeting us, too."

"Five or ten minutes won't hurt," Nicki pointed out. She lowered her voice. "It'd be rude to refuse and besides, the lady is right. Christine looks a little pale."

"I still feel a little shaky," Christine admitted. "Lemonade does sounds good."

Laura propped the bicycles against the wrought-iron fence at the front of the house and followed Christine and Nicki up the stairs. "Your home is lovely," she told Mrs. Greaves. "It looks just like a gingerbread house. And pink is one of my favorite colors."

Mrs. Greaves beamed and patted young Laura on the shoulder. "Mine, too."

Two

Nicki had never seen a more comfortable spot than Mrs. Greaves's kitchen. Colorful knickknacks filled every available space on the walls, and the gleaming white floor and spotless countertops gave the place a cheery, open feeling. Buttons sat in a blue-and-white gingham dog bed by the back door.

"My mother would love this kitchen," Nicki said, sitting at the table. "She sells real estate and she's always saying that a pretty kitchen is the most important thing in a house."

"I like it," Mrs. Greaves said, handing each of the girls a tall glass of lemonade. "After my husband died I was able to completely renovate the house and redecorate in more contemporary colors. The original colors were rather drab." She paused. "The work gave me something to do, and it's good for an older woman to keep busy."

Christine shifted her gaze from the cookie jar to their hostess. "Have you lived here long?"

"All my life." Mrs. Greaves passed around a plate of cookies. "I was born in the nursery upstairs. The only time I haven't lived here was when I went to college in Virginia." She nodded toward the cookies. "You girls need to eat up. You need your energy."

When they had all taken a cookie, Mrs. Greaves lowered the plate. "I didn't finish college, though, because my parents became ill. Because I was their only child, I came home to nurse them. When they died, the house became mine. Fortunately, I married a

6

man who loved this place as much as I do, and we raised our daughter here. Our grandchild lived here a while, too, but I don't see him as much as I'd like to . . . not anymore."

When Mrs. Greaves paused, Nicki sensed that they had stumbled onto a painful topic. "Um, do you have any great-grand-children?" she asked.

Mrs. Greaves shook her head. "Not yet. Howard is certainly old enough to settle down and get married, but he can't seem to hold onto a job, much less a wife."

"I may never get married," Christine said. "After college I'm either going to open a day-care center or a veterinary hospital. I know all about taking care of kids and I love taking care of dogs. Who knows?" She took a bite of cookie and munched thoughtfully. "I could open a doggie day-care center."

"That is a wonderful idea," Mrs. Greaves said, smiling. "I hate to leave Buttons alone when I go out. I used to have two dogs, Buttons and Bows, but Bows died two years ago. Now Buttons is unbearably lonely whenever I'm not around, so I don't go out much at all."

Nicki grinned. "Our dog doesn't care whether we're home or not," she said. "Stooge is a bloodhound, and all he does is lie around like a piece of carpet. The only time he moves is to go eat or go outside. Dad says he's a great hunting dog, but he's about as lively as a pair of worn-out bedroom slippers."

Mrs. Greaves passed the plate of cookies again. "And what is your ambition, Nicki?"

Nicki blushed. "It may sound silly, but I want to play a piano concert at Carnegie Hall."

"She could do it," Christine told Mrs. Greaves. "She has perfect pitch and plays piano beautifully."

Mrs. Greaves lifted a silver brow. "Really?"

The telephone rang, and Nicki nodded. "Yep. Your phone rings on a B flat."

"My goodness." Mrs. Greaves gave them a smile and pushed away from the table. "Excuse me. It isn't every day I hear that."

After Mrs. Greaves stepped into the hall to answer the phone, Nicki lowered her voice and looked at her friends. "What's so exciting about knowing your phone rings on a B flat?"

"Shhh," Christine said. "Listen."

Though Nicki didn't really want to eavesdrop on the woman's phone call, Mrs. Greaves spoke so loudly it was hard to ignore what she was saying. After greeting her caller with a bright voice, the old woman sighed. "I'm sorry," she said, "but I'm afraid you have reached a wrong number. Good-bye."

After a moment, she returned to the kitchen and smiled at the girls. "I'm afraid those cookies weren't enough to bring color back to your friend's cheeks. Would you like me to mix up some brownies?" She turned and opened the door to her pantry. "Howard always said my brownies were the best in Pine Grove."

Nicki glanced at the others. "I'm afraid we ought to be running along. We're supposed to meet a friend who lives in the apartments behind your house."

Some of the eagerness disappeared from Mrs. Greaves's face, but she smiled as she stepped closer to the girls. "Are you sure you're well enough, sweetheart?" She ran her hand lightly over Christine's red hair. "I'd hate to see you go outside and faint in the street."

"I'm not really the fainting type," Christine said, laughing. "I'll be fine. And thank you for the cookies and lemonade."

The girls stood and placed their dishes in the sink while Mrs. Greaves protested and said she didn't expect company to clean up after themselves. As they walked through her spotless foyer, Nicki noticed a collection of family photographs hanging on the wall.

She pointed to an old black-and-white photograph in a simple frame. "Is this your family?"

"Yes." Mrs. Greaves smiled. "Can't you tell that thing is as ancient as I am? Those are my grandparents on the porch of this house when it was built in 1861, the year the Civil War began. Building was slow, hard work because materials weren't available during the war like they were during peace time."

"Wow—look at how old these pictures and frames are," Laura said. She whistled. "I'll bet some of these frames would be worth a fortune to an antiques dealer."

"Doesn't matter," Mrs. Greaves said, "because I'd never sell them. They are part of my life, my history, and the history of this house. As long as I'm living, I want everything to stay together just as it is. Many of the furnishings in this house have aged over a hundred years without ever moving from the spot they're in."

Nicki pointed to an old schoolhouse clock by the foot of the stairs. "That's a beautiful clock. My grandmother had one like it."

Mrs. Greaves chuckled and clasped her hands. "That clock was old when my granddaddy bought it. It was made in 1802, and it will probably tick on for another two hundred years if taken care of. They made things to last in those days, girls. Just look at me." Smiling, she lifted a shoulder in a shrug. "I'm eighty years old and still ticking like a trooper."

Nicki grinned. "Wow," she said, not knowing what else to say. "Congratulations."

Mrs. Greaves shook her head. "Don't congratulate me for doing what comes natural. If you live right, eat right, and think right, you'll live long. That's what the Good Book says." She paused to open the front door. "Now you girls had better get along. You don't want to keep your friend waiting."

As they filed out, Mrs. Greaves called, "Please come again. Buttons and I would love to see you."

"I'd love to come," Christine said, surprising Laura and Nicki. "I can't speak for anyone else, but will you be home tomorrow afternoon? I could come by after church."

Mrs. Greaves smiled and patted her apron. "That would be nice. You are all welcome, of course. I'll look forward to it, and I'll make brownies."

—

"'Bout time you guys got here," Meredith said when the three girls wheeled their bikes up to Mr. Dixon's apartment. She pretended to be irritated until she heard about Christine's accident and Mrs. Greaves's hospitality.

The girls settled into deck chairs around the apartment complex's pool. "You mean that woman has lived in that house for eighty years?" Meredith asked, shading her eyes from the sun. "My dad's been living in this apartment for three years and I never even knew anybody lived in that house. It's always quiet over there."

"We should have crashed into her hedge sooner," Nicki said. "She's pretty cool."

"I love her," Christine said. "Both sets of my grandparents live in other states. Mrs. Greaves is like the grandmother I've always wanted."

"You're just flattered because she called you sweetheart," Laura said, teasing.

Christine blushed. "Maybe, but that's not the only reason. She bakes, she likes dogs, and I'll bet she could teach me to make quilts or something. That's what grandmothers are supposed to do."

Nicki laughed. "Not anymore. One of my grandmothers manages a health spa."

"My grandmother runs a corporation," Laura said.

"My grandmother lives in Korea," Kim said. "I miss her very much."

"My grandmother," Meredith said, "is president of a university. So what's the point? Are you saying we should all trade in our grandmothers for someone like Mrs. Greaves? What's she supposed to do, adopt all of us?"

Christine snapped her fingers. "Maybe we could adopt *her!* I know she's lonely. Did you hear how disappointed she was when the phone call was a wrong number?"

"Christine is right," Laura said, nodding. "Her only company is a dog. I'm willing to stop by and see her."

"She's interesting," Nicki said. "She knows about history and houses and antiques. Next year we have to take American history and I'll bet we could get extra credit by talking to Mrs. Greaves about how things *really* were in the old days."

Meredith shrugged. "If she's as sharp as you say—"

"She is," Christine said.

"Well, okay." Meredith frowned. "Old people have always freaked me out a little. They look funny, they smell funny, and honestly, sometimes they jabber on about things that make no sense! I met my great-grandmother at my cousin's wedding and had to introduce myself three times! Each time she'd smile and say, 'And whose daughter are you?'"

Christine lifted her chin. "Mrs. Greaves isn't like that."

Kim, who had been quietly trailing her fingertips in the pool, spoke up. "I would like to meet this woman," she said. "I am lonely for my grandmother. Perhaps a new friendship will help both of us."

Nicki nodded. "Okay, it's settled. Tomorrow afternoon we'll go visit her again. Meredith, this time we'll meet here first, okay? I think you'll really like Mrs. Greaves. Laura, Chris, and I will introduce you and Kim and you'll see how neat she is.

Maybe we can make it a weekly tradition."

"As long as we're back by five o'clock," Meredith said. "My mom comes to pick me up at five." She shook her head. "She won't believe I've spent my Sunday afternoon visiting an old lady."

"We'll be back by five," Nicki promised. "We don't want to wear out our welcome."

"Just one thing," Laura said, smiling at Meredith. "We're traveling in the car, not by bike, I'll have our driver pick Christine and Nicki up, and we'll meet you and Kim here at the apartment. I don't want Christine to take a chance on breaking her neck again!"

Three

The next afternoon, Mr. Peterson, the Cushmans' chauffeur, dropped Laura, Nicki, and Christine in front of Meredith's father's apartment. Meredith and Kim were waiting in lounge chairs by the pool.

"Laura, call me if you need a ride home," the grandfatherly driver called through the open window.

Laura patted her purse. "Got my cell phone. Thanks, Mr. Peterson."

"See, Meredith?" Nicki called. "We didn't stop to have any adventures without you." When Meredith didn't answer, Nicki looked at Kim. "What's wrong?"

Kim's eyes were troubled. "Meredith is upset. She heard bad news this afternoon."

Nicki pulled up a chair. "What happened, Meredith?"

Meredith looked up and tried to smile. "I don't know why I'm so upset. I guess I knew it was coming, but now that it's here, it sort of took me by surprise."

Christine frowned. "What took you by surprise?"

"My parents are filing for divorce."

After a moment of heavy silence, Laura shook her head. "I thought your parents were already divorced. Hasn't your father been living in this apartment for ages?"

Meredith nodded. "Yeah. My parents have been separated for three years and I guess we've all adjusted to that. Or I adjusted. My older brother Steve and his wife live on the beach and they never even see Mom and Dad. My sister Dana is married, so this won't really bother her. And I'm used to spending the week with Mom and the weekends with Dad. But even then I had a mother and father who were married to each other. Now I won't have that."

"You still have a mother and father," Kim said, her voice soft. "They both love you still."

"You'll keep spending the week with your mom and weekends with your dad, right?" Christine asked. "So nothing will change there, will it?"

Meredith gave her a weak smile. "Dad even made a joke and said nothing would change except his income tax filing status."

"Then why are they getting a divorce?" Laura asked.

Meredith sighed. "I don't know. Maybe they just don't want to be married anymore. When Dad first moved out of the house, I thought maybe they'd work out their problems and he'd come home. I guess they figured if they couldn't work things out in three years, they might as well go ahead with the divorce."

Nicki looked at her friend and tried to imagine what she must be feeling. Meredith always seemed to have everything together; Nicki had never seen her this upset.

"I'm really sorry, Meredith," Nicki said. "I can't imagine what you're going through."

"I lost my father altogether when he died," Laura said. "At least you still have your dad."

"This may be difficult for your heart," Kim said, smiling, "but your head will see the way."

Nicki caught Meredith's eye and knew she was about to roll her eyes. Kim had a philosophical way of looking at things that was utterly foreign to practical, down-to-earth Meredith.

Meredith stood up. "Thanks for trying to help. I'll be fine, I know I will. I just have to get used to the idea of having parents who are divorced. Somehow it wasn't so bad when they were separated, but I guess they haven't been married for a long time."

"I know what will cheer you up," Christine said, standing. "Mrs. Greaves's brownies. Come on, she's expecting us."

—

As the girls filed through the gate at the apartment pool, Christine pointed to a break in the hedge at the boundary of Mrs. Greaves's backyard. "Look, we can slip in through here. We're friends now, so let's just go to the back door."

As they walked across the back lawn, Nicki could see that the kitchen door stood open behind the screen door. A delicious aroma drifted by on the breeze. "Umm, I can smell those brownies," she said. "I hope she uses walnuts in her recipe."

"I like mine with chocolate chips," Meredith said. She gave Nicki a smile that said she was trying her best to be cheerful.

"Our cook makes brownies with marshmallow cream centers," Laura said, her eyes rolling in delight. "They are heavenly!"

Christine led the way up the short staircase to the back porch, but then she stopped and put her finger to her lips. "Listen!" she whispered as the others drew near.

A man's angry voice echoed in the house and reached the girls outside. "You're a foolish, silly old woman!" he yelled. "And one of these days you'll realize how wrong you are to oppose me. Just you wait, old lady, you'll be sorry!"

The front screen door slammed with a bang and Nicki stood on tiptoe to peek through the kitchen window. Through the narrow hallway she had a clear view of the front door, but all she could see was the back of a man's head and shoulders as he marched down the front steps to the sidewalk. He was dressed in a gray shirt and had dark, wavy hair.

The inside of the house was gloomy, but as Nicki's eyes adjusted she saw Mrs. Greaves huddled against the front screen door, her back to Nicki. Her shoulders shook slightly, as if she were crying. Buttons danced at her feet, and even from where she stood Nicki could hear him growling.

"I think she's crying," Nicki whispered to the other girls. "Wait a minute before you knock, Christine. We don't want her to know we heard that. It might embarrass her."

Laura put her hand on Nicki's shoulder. "Who do you think that awful man was?"

Nicki shrugged. "Could have been anybody. A bill collector, a lawyer, a relative, a friend—"

"Could have been her grandson, Howard," Laura said, her eyes wide. "Can you imagine anybody being so mean to their grandmother?"

Christine shook her head. "I don't think it was her grandson. Mrs. Greaves likes her grandson. I could never like anybody that mean."

"Okay," Nicki said. "Let's knock and maybe we'll find out who it was."

Christine stood in the back doorway and knocked loudly on the screen door's wooden frame. "Mrs. Greaves? We're here."

A moment later Mrs. Greaves came to the back door, as pleasant and bright-eyed as she had been the day before. Buttons leaped at her feet, yapping a friendly greeting.

"Goodness, girls, you get prettier every day! How are you, Laura? It's good to see you again, Nicki. How's the head, Christine? Still wobbly from your fall?"

Christine gave Mrs. Greaves an affectionate hug and stooped to pat Buttons. Mrs. Greaves smiled at Kim and Meredith. "Hello there. I'm so glad you've come. Nicki, who are these other two pretty girls?"

Nicki remembered her manners. "Sorry—let me introduce Meredith Dixon and Kim Park. Meredith is probably the smartest kid in the county and Kim has recently come to this country from Korea. Her mother had a kidney transplant last month."

Mrs. Greaves gave Kim a concerned smile. "I hope your mother is doing well."

Kim bowed respectfully. "Very well, thank you. We are grateful for American hospitals and an American kidney donor."

"Well, come on in." Mrs. Greaves stepped back and welcomed the girls into the kitchen. "First I'm going to give each of you a warm brownie, then I want to hear the latest news. I really enjoy the company of young folks like you."

Christine gave Nicki a pointed look. This was the perfect time to find out who that nasty visitor had been . . .

Christine rose to the challenge. "Do you have much company, Mrs. Greaves?" she asked.

Mrs. Greaves pulled a large pan out of the oven. "Well, no, I don't usually. I used to belong to a ladies' group at my church; we met every Saturday morning for a nice brunch. But my arthritis has been flaring up and I can't walk down to the restaurant as easily as I used to. But they were women my age and there's just nothing like being with young people. They're the key to staying young at heart, I always say."

She pointed to the pan. "In the upper right corner you'll find my chewy fudge brownies with pecans. In the lower right corner I used walnuts instead of pecans, and in the upper left corner I used . . ." She frowned and stared off into space.

Meredith looked at Nicki. *See*, the look said. *I told you old people couldn't remember anything.*

"What did I use? Oh yes, I believe those are the chocolate chip brownies."

Nicki cast a ha-ha glance at Meredith. "Chocolate chip are Meredith's favorite," she said.

"In the lower left corner, I marbled the brownies with marshmallow cream," Mrs. Greaves finished. "What kind would you like, Christine? You can pick your favorite."

"Pecan, please." Christine smiled and held up her napkin. "They all look delicious. You shouldn't have gone to all this trouble."

"Nonsense." Mrs. Greaves lifted out a brownie and served it to Christine. "Nothing is too much trouble for good friends."

Even though Meredith complained at least once or twice about visiting an old lady, every Sunday afternoon for the next three weeks the girls met at Mr. Dixon's apartment, ducked through the hedge, climbed the porch steps, and knocked on Mrs. Greaves's back door. And every week Mrs. Greaves shared her home, her endless supply of stories, and her brownies.

"I've gained five pounds since we met you," Nicki teased her one afternoon. "And Mr. Peterson said to tell you that your peanut butter brownies are the best he's ever had."

Mrs. Greaves chuckled as she poured tall glasses of ice-cold lemonade. "You'll have to thank him for me," she said, pulling up a chair next to Christine. "By the way . . . is your Mr. Peterson a bachelor?"

Laura caught Nicki's eye, then giggled. "Do you want us to set you up with him?"

"Heavens, no," Mrs. Greaves said, laughing. "Although it would be nice to have someone drive me around town. I'm perfectly happy just the way I am. Which reminds me, I want to share something with you girls." She reached for a magazine on the kitchen counter, pulled it to the table, and pointed to a chart. "Do you see this?"

Meredith lowered her brownie to peer at the chart. "Projected Life Expectancy," she read. "What is that?"

"You girls have a projected life expectancy of about eighty-four years," Mrs. Greaves said. "That's wonderful. When I was born, a girl's life expectancy was only sixty-one years."

"Then you've beaten the odds," Meredith said. "You're eighty, right?"

Mrs. Greaves nodded, but the smile left her lips as she pointed to a row on the chart. "I was looking at this chart yesterday and I suddenly realized that I have very few years left. According to statistics, I could drop dead at any minute." She burst out in a short laugh and tapped her forehead. "With this headache, I'm tempted to believe it."

Christine reached out to pat the old woman's hand. "Don't even think like that, Mrs. G. You're in good health, aren't you?"

"I always thought I was. Then again, I always thought I would live forever. But yesterday I realized that I could probably count my remaining years on the fingers of one hand. And that, girls, is a sobering thought."

Nicki sat quietly as the truth of Mrs. Greaves's words sank in. How would it feel to know that long-range plans were out of the question? That in two or three or four years, life could be over, even for someone as alive and vibrant as Mrs. Greaves?

The woman smiled again. "I want to ask you something, Christine." She reached for a chain around her neck, then pulled the chain up and over her head. From the end of the chain dangled a skeleton key. Her hand shook slightly as she handed the key and chain to Christine. "I wondered what would happen to my sweet little Buttons if anything were to happen to me. This is a skeleton key that will lock and unlock any door in this house except the front door—my son-in-law made me put a modern lock on the front door, but every other lock in the house is still old-fashioned. Anyway, will you take this key and look after Buttons if"—she hesitated—"well, if the need should ever arise?"

Christine took the key and nodded. "Sure, Mrs. G. I'd be glad to. But nothing's going to happen to you."

"The chain is 14-karat, so it won't turn your neck green." Mrs. Greaves laughed and stood. "Now, who is still hungry?"

Meredith held up her empty plate. "I think we all are."

Mrs. Greaves picked up her spatula and cut a walnut brownie. "Who wants to try—"

Without warning, Mrs. Greaves slumped over and fell. The brownie flew across the table and the spatula clattered across the white tile. Nicki heard a dull thud when the woman's head hit the floor.

Christine gasped and Laura screamed. Meredith stared, then spilled out of her chair and knelt beside Mrs. Greaves. Nicki slipped to the woman's other side while Kim grabbed Buttons, who had begun to bark and scramble in confusion.

Nicki looked at Meredith. "What happened?"

Meredith shook her head. "Chris, grab the phone and call 911. Hurry!"

Nicki tried to remember what she'd heard in her first-aid class. "Laura, can you look for a blanket?" Laura didn't wait, but ran out of the kitchen. An instant later Nicki heard her feet pounding on the stairs.

Meredith studied Mrs. Greaves's face, which had been pale but was rapidly flushing with color. "Kim, can you run over and get my dad? He's home reading. Tell him to hurry!"

Kim dropped Buttons into his dog bed, then slammed out the door without a word. From the hallway, Nicki could hear Christine's voice: "Hello? I'd like to report an emergency. Address? 616 River Road? Yeah, that sounds right. It's the pink house next to the intersection with Palm Avenue."

"Stay calm, Christine," Meredith called. She looked at Nicki as she placed her fingertips on Mrs. Greaves's thin wrist. "This is another reason why I don't like old people—they're always sick!"

"Not always," Nicki whispered, but she knew Meredith was more frightened than serious.

Christine stuck her head into the room. "Our friend," she said, speaking into the phone, "she was talking to us and suddenly she fell down. Is she breathing?" She looked at Nicki. "Is she?"

"Yes," Nicki called, "but her breathing isn't normal. It sounds like she's snoring."

"She's sort of snoring," Christine told the emergency operator. "Just a minute, let me ask. Is she pale?"

"No," Meredith answered. "She's flushed. And I found a pulse. It's not strong, but she has one."

"She's red in the face," Christine told the operator. "And she has a pulse. So are you guys coming or not?"

She hung up the phone and ran back into the kitchen. "She said they've already sent someone. They'll be here any minute."

Laura's feet thumped on the stairs and a minute later she appeared in the kitchen, her arms filled with a quilt. "This was the first thing I found," she said. "Should we cover her?"

"Yes, but we can't move her," Meredith said, stepping back. "We have to keep her warm, but we have to leave room for the paramedics to work."

While Laura spread the quilt over Mrs. Greaves's body, Christine knelt and held the old woman's hand. "Hang in there, Mrs. G," she said. "We're here with you. We're going to take care of you."

Nicki tilted her head as the sound of a siren caught her attention. Soon she heard steps on the porch, then a team of paramedics stormed into the kitchen. The girls moved out of the way as Mr. Dixon and Kim joined them on the back porch.

Mr. Dixon was out of breath from running. "Is everything under control?"

Meredith told her father what little they knew, and they all watched as the paramedics gave Mrs. Greaves oxygen, then put her on a gurney and wheeled her to the ambulance.

Nicki trailed behind the last paramedic to leave the house. "What do you think happened?" she asked. "Will she be all right?"

The woman glanced at her. "Looks like a cerebrovascular accident," she said. "CVAs are common in older folks. Sorry, I can't say anything more until we get her to the hospital."

Nicki returned to the others. "I wish she'd speak English. What's a CVA?"

"A stroke," Meredith said, her voice quiet. "A blood vessel in the brain bursts and causes brain damage. My grandpa had one last year."

Nicki looked at her friend. "And how's he—"

"He died," Meredith said, cutting her off.

Nicki noticed Mr. Dixon was quiet, watching the paramedics as they loaded the gurney. Was he thinking of his father?

"I'm sorry, Mr. Dixon," she said.

He looked at her and smiled. "It's okay. These things happen."

"I want to go with Mrs. Greaves," Christine said, handing Buttons to Kim. "Nicki, will you call my mom and let her know what's happening?"

Nicki peered at her friend. "Are you sure you want to do this? She could die, you know."

Christine bit her lip and nodded. "I don't want her to be alone." She waved at the others, then hurried toward the ambulance.

Nicki glanced at the old schoolhouse clock. Only ten minutes earlier they had been talking and eating brownies in the kitchen. She had never realized that an eternity could pass in ten minutes.

Four

Mr. Dixon looked at Laura, Meredith, Kim, and Nicki. "I'm not sure what we should do now," he said. "I suppose we should contact someone in her family."

"I don't think she has any family," Nicki said. "Only a grandson, Howard Somebody. We don't know his last name."

"She had friends at her church, but she hasn't seen them in over a year," Meredith remembered. "But maybe her pastor can help."

"We were her friends, if only for a little while," said Kim. "It is our responsibility to help."

Nicki noticed that Meredith's brow had wrinkled as it always did when something bothered her. "Dad," she said, turning to her father, "she was just talking about dying. Do you think she knew this was going to happen?"

Mr. Dixon rubbed Meredith's shoulder. "I don't know, honey. Doctors say there are some warnings of an impending stroke, but I don't know if this lady experienced any warning signs."

Nicki remembered the angry man they had seen leaving the house a few weeks before. Had he been back?

She looked at Mr. Dixon. "Could an emotional upset trigger a stroke? Like if someone made you really mad about something?"

Mr. Dixon smiled. "I'm a professor, Nicki, not a doctor. Sorry, but I don't know. What I do know, though, is that I'm proud of all of you. Mrs. Greaves should be thankful you were here. If she had been alone, she might have died right there on her kitchen floor. Your fast thinking probably saved her life."

"Why don't you go on home, Dad," Meredith said. "We'll clean up the mess in the kitchen and feed the dog. I'll be home in a little bit."

Mr. Dixon said good-bye, then walked slowly down the back porch steps. When he had gone, Meredith wiped a tear from her eye. "My grandfather did die all alone because no one was there to help," she told the other girls. "My dad has a hard time with that."

Nicki nodded, then led the way back into the kitchen. "Well, we have a lot to do. We need to clean up this food and wash these dishes, then we should try to find an address book or something with the names and phone numbers of any family Mrs. Greaves might have—especially her grandson. After that, I guess we should feed Buttons and lock the house."

"Okay." Meredith gave Nicki a tired smile. "I warned you that old people could be trouble."

Laura filled the sink with warm soapy water while Meredith gathered up the dirty dishes. Kim covered the leftover brownies with plastic wrap she found in a cupboard.

Nicki looked around the kitchen. "Where would I put my address book if I were Mrs. Greaves?"

"Most people keep one near the phone," Laura suggested.

"If it isn't there, see if she has a desk," Meredith added. "I thought I saw an antique desk in the living room."

Nicki stepped out to the hall where the telephone hung on the wall. Nothing here—no notepad, no phone numbers. She crept quietly down the hall, placing her steps on the hall runner instead of the polished wooden floors. Funny, how scary and empty the once-friendly house seemed now that its owner had gone away.

The living room reminded Nicki of a museum. An elegant sofa with silken cushions and polished wooden legs sat regally in front of the fireplace. Two beautiful wing chairs faced each other near a dainty table covered with a lace doily and a collection of tiny pictures in matching silver frames. A small drawer had been cut in the front of the table. Nicki felt like a snoop as she pulled it open.

"Forgive me, Mrs. Greaves," she whispered, "but I'm only trying to help." Nothing in the drawer but an old photograph, its silver frame dark with tarnish. The photo showed two little girls with curly hair. Wearing lace dresses, they held hands and smiled at the camera.

Nicki was surprised. Of all the old pictures on the desk and in the foyer, these were the first two smiles she'd seen.

She slipped the picture back into the drawer and slid it back into place. A tall secretary occupied the far corner of the room, set off by the dainty chair placed in front of it. Nicki walked over to examine the antique more closely.

One side of the secretary reminded Nicki of a china closet—it had shelves and a glass-paned door. Inside, on the shelves, stood a collection of fragile teacups and matching saucers.

The other side of the secretary featured a shelf and a pull-down desk. The desk was up, locked into position, and a tiny skeleton key rested in the lock.

Nicki felt like a genuine snoop as she carefully turned the key and pulled down the desk. She gasped when the piece revealed its contents.

Inside the compartment's several cubbyholes were cards of all types—Christmas cards, birthday cards, valentines, anniversary cards, sympathy cards, and get-well cards. Nicki pulled out the contents of one compartment and looked through the collection of notes.

"To my darling Lela, from your loving husband Alden" . . . a valentine, dated 1945.

"With prayers and deep sympathy, from the congregation of Pine Grove Congregational Church," dated 1953. A feminine hand had written only one word beneath the note: Alden.

"Flowers and candy cannot express my love for you, Mother" . . . a Mother's Day card, signed by Mary Alice and dated May 13, 1953.

"With prayers and deep sympathy, from the congregation of Pine Grove Congregational Church," dated November 1987, and underneath a woman had written "Robert and Mary Alice."

Why, Mrs. Greaves's entire life was in these cards! Nicki called to the others: "Hey, come look at this!"

Meredith was the first to reach her. "Did you find anything?"

"I found a lot, but not what we're looking for." Nicki pointed to the cards. "Look at this—a valentine from Alden in 1945. Alden must have been her husband."

Meredith did some quick calculations in her head. "Makes sense. Mrs. Greaves would have been twenty in 1945. It's likely she was married by then."

"Here's a sympathy card from her church. Apparently Alden died in 1953."

"She was a young widow," Laura said. "Just like my mother."

"She saved a Mother's Day card from her daughter, Mary Alice, but Mary Alice and someone named Robert died in 1987."

Meredith nodded. "Mrs. Greaves was sixty-two that year, but that doesn't tell us how old Mary Alice was or who Robert was."

"I'm sure we could find out," Nicki said, pointing to the other card-stuffed compartments. "Mrs. Greaves likes to save things. There are probably birth announcements, wedding invitations, and anything else we would need in here."

"If Mary Alice was her only child, then Robert was probably her husband," she said. "They died together, somehow, and their child survived."

"That would be Howard." Meredith drew in her breath. "This is sad stuff. No wonder Mrs. Greaves likes having people around. I'd go nuts living here alone with nothing more than memories around me. I wonder why she doesn't move into a condo or a retirement home?"

"Why, how could you suggest such a thing?" Laura whirled, gesturing to the furnishings in the living room. "Her whole life is in this house! This place has character! Why would she want to leave this and move into a modern, ugly condo?"

"Well," Nicki said, putting the cards back into their spot, "unless she has an address book upstairs, she must have memorized any phone numbers she needs to call. There's no address book here."

"But this is fascinating." Laura smiled as Nicki locked the desk. "When my father died, we didn't have anything like that stuff to remember him by. Mrs. Greaves has her entire family history in one piece of furniture!"

"We'll have to come back tomorrow and keep looking," Nicki said. "For now, we should feed Buttons and get him settled. I guess he's used to going in and out of his doggie door, so at least we don't have to worry about letting him in and out."

"Before we go," Kim said, "can we call the hospital and check on Mrs. Greaves's condition?"

Nicki nodded, but she was almost afraid to make the call. Mrs. Greaves had looked so near death lying there on the floor . . .

"Okay," Nicki said, "but Kim, you should call. You're more comfortable around hospitals than the rest of us."

"You'd better use one of your voices," Meredith said. Meredith and the other girls were constantly amazed at Kim's ability to mimic voices. "If you sound like a kid they won't give you a straight answer."

"Use the voice of the lady paramedic," Laura suggested. "She sounded really professional."

Kim dialed the phone. "Hello? Emergency room, please." She waited, then spoke again. "I'd like to check on the status of Mrs. Lela Greaves," she said in the paramedic's voice. "She was brought in with a CVA." She nodded. "Wasn't there a girl with her? Is she available?"

Kim paused a moment, then spoke in her own voice. "Christine? It's Kim. How is Mrs. Greaves?"

Kim listened, then placed her hand over the receiver and looked at Nicki and the others. "She says Mrs. Greaves is stable and out of danger, but she is still unconscious. Christine asks if we called her mother to let her know where she was. She will need a ride home from the hospital."

Nicki gulped. "I forgot to call. Tell Christine I'll call her mom right away."

After Kim hung up, Nicki dialed Christine's number. When Mrs. Kelshaw answered, Nicki could hear the sounds of a busy household in the background.

"Mrs. Kelshaw, Christine wanted me to call and let you know she needs a ride home," Nicki began.

Mrs. Kelshaw was a no-nonsense mother. "Nicki, Christine knows she's not supposed to call and tell me anything. She usually understands that she must *ask*."

"But this is different."

After Nicki explained Mrs. Greaves's accident, understanding flowed into Mrs. Kelshaw's voice. "Of course, we'll pick her up at the hospital. You girls did a mighty fine thing. Just be sure to lock the house up tight. You all had better head home now. It's nearly dark outside."

Nicki hung up and looked at the others. "We'd better go now. But maybe we can stop by the hospital and see Mrs. Greaves tomorrow."

Everyone but Meredith nodded.

"She's such a sweet old lady," Laura said as they filed out the front door. "I'd love to help her if I can."

"I never thought of her as sickly," Nicki said, testing the lock. "She seemed to be able to handle everything around here."

"In Korea, grandparents are given much respect," Kim said. "The white head is envied."

"I wish my mother felt that way," Meredith said, crossing the front porch and moving down the front steps. "She found a gray hair last week and nearly had a fit."

Five

Laura arranged for Mr. Peterson to give the girls a ride to the hospital after school on Monday.

"I called the hospital after lunch and they said Mrs. Greaves is conscious and stable," Christine said. "That's good news."

Meredith pulled out a notebook. "I did some research in the library during my study hall and I found out what we can expect when we see her. Some strokes are serious, even deadly, but if Mrs. Greaves is stable, she will probably be fine. But often strokes cause paralysis of one side of the body. They can also cause a loss of speech or a loss of memory."

Nicki shook her head. "You mean Mrs. Greaves may not even remember us? We were with her just yesterday!"

Meredith shrugged. "It all depends on where the blood clot in the brain was located. It could have ruptured in a memory center or a motor skills center or a speech center. Or maybe in some place the doctors don't even understand yet."

"That's great," Christine muttered, looking out the window. "My adopted grandmother may not even know who I am now."

"We should wait and see," Kim reminded them. "There is no reason to worry about what may not be."

The girls slipped past the visitor's desk in the hospital lobby. "Act like you know what you're doing and no one will stop us," Meredith commanded. "They don't usually allow kids in the rooms, but we can pretend we're going to the cafeteria or the gift shop."

"Maybe they'll think we're volunteers," Laura said. "I've always wanted to be a candy striper."

"You have to be fifteen," Christine said. "My sister was a candy striper for three days. She quit when some kid threw up on her."

As the girls turned a corner, they saw two nurses standing in the hallway. The older nurse, who wore a badge labeled "Supervisor," frowned and shook her finger at the younger nurse. "You really don't know how to do your job," the supervisor snapped. "Being careful is one thing, being overcareful is another. Always ask yourself, 'Is this best for the patient?' Use your common sense, nurse!"

Laura made a face as they hurried by the nurses. "You know, maybe I don't want to be a candy striper after all."

The duty nurse on Mrs. Greaves's floor pressed her lips together when the girls stopped at the desk. "No way can I let you in to see her," she said, crossing her arms. "We allow only two visitors at a time, and those visitors must be over sixteen. I don't know how you girls made it up to this floor, but you can turn right around and get back on the elevator."

"But we're her only friends," Christine said, leaning on the counter. "She doesn't have any relatives but a grandson, and we don't know how to reach him."

"It's terribly important that we see Mrs. Greaves," Meredith added in her most mature voice. "You see, I'm doing research on cerebrovascular accidents and I need to compare—"

"You can compare over there." The nurse pointed to the elevator. "Now run along, all of you."

Nicki elbowed Kim. "Do something, quick!"

Kim glanced over her shoulder, where the nurse had gone back to her work. After nodding at Nicki, Kim left the other girls and slipped around the corner, out of sight.

Nicki led the others to the elevator and waited.

"Nurse!" Kim snapped in the voice of the nursing supervisor.

The duty nurse snapped to attention and looked up, but all she could see was the group of girls.

"Let those girls visit the patient," Kim continued, speaking in the older woman's voice. "Being careful is one thing, but being overcareful is another. Is this best for the patient? Use your common sense, nurse!"

The duty nurse wrinkled her brow and peered around the corner, then nodded. "Yes, Mrs. Calhoun," she said, sighing. She looked at the girls, then pointed to the long hallway. "Okay," she whispered, "but only two of you in the room at a time, and only for five minutes each."

The girls grinned at each other as Kim rejoined them, then they confidently followed the nurse into Mrs. Greaves's room.

◄—

The head of Mrs. Greaves's bed had been raised so she could look out the window. One bottle dripped clear liquid into a tube that ran to Mrs. Greaves's left wrist. A small machine on a cart beeped with each beat of Mrs. Greaves's heart. Nicki felt like she had walked into a television movie. Surely at any moment the beeps would stop, the nurse would yell, and all sorts of confusion would break loose . . .

But nothing happened. The nurse announced, "Visitors for you, Mrs. Greaves," in a cheery voice, but the older woman didn't even turn her head. She murmured something, though, words Nicki couldn't hear.

Christine reached for the old woman's free hand. "Did you say something, Mrs. Greaves? Do you remember me? It's Christine."

Mrs. Greaves's hand trembled as Christine held it. Finally her head turned and she looked first at Christine, then at Nicki. Nicki shuddered. The lower left corner of Mrs. Greaves's mouth drooped, and her left eye was half-closed.

"Peaches," Mrs. Greaves whispered. "Peaches."

Chris looked at Nicki. "Did she say peaches?"

Nicki leaned forward. "Don't you mean Buttons? He's at your house and we're taking care of him until you get home. You don't have to worry about Buttons."

Mrs. Greaves turned away and looked toward the window. "Peaches," she repeated.

Nicki jumped when the door opened. A doctor entered, but he didn't seem to think it unusual to find two girls in the room. "Good afternoon," he said, all business as he looked at the chart in his hand. "It looks like your grandmother will be fine, if she wants to be."

Christine began to correct him. "Oh, but she's not—"

"What do you mean, if she wants to be?" Nicki asked.

The doctor lowered his clipboard and looked Nicki in the eye. "Well, young lady, a lot of older people can't see much sense in getting well. We have a series of exercises for Mrs. Greaves that will help her regain the use of her left side, but until she's willing to do them, they won't do her any good. The slight paralysis you see here isn't permanent."

Christine's eyes opened wide. "She's paralyzed?"

"Only partially, and only on one side," the doctor explained. "Your grandmother was lucky—the stroke could have been a lot worse. If you girls can convince her to get better, she'll be fine."

Nicki looked over at Mrs. Greaves's beautiful silver hair. "She's not our grandmother. We sort of adopted her. But she doesn't seem to know us anymore, so I don't think we can help."

The doctor leaned forward and peered at his patient. "Mrs. Greaves, do you know where you are?"

"Peaches," she replied.

The doctor shrugged. "Apparently she has experienced some memory loss. If I were you, I'd get the lady some peaches and make her happy. Then she'll have a better chance of getting well."

He turned and walked out as suddenly as he had come in.

"Peaches?" Nicki asked. "Where are we going to find peaches in November?"

Christine shook her head, then gave Mrs. Greaves's hand another squeeze. "We'll see you later, Mrs. G." She leaned forward and kissed the woman on the cheek. "I love you."

—

An hour later they had gathered again on Mrs. Greaves's back porch. "Are you sure this is all right?" Laura asked. "We're not trespassing, are we?"

"She gave Christine a key," Nicki reminded her. "We're not going to take anything and we're not snooping for material to hurt anybody. We're only trying to bring her whatever she wants—peaches."

Christine turned the skeleton key in the old lock. The rusty tumbler turned and the door opened.

Nicki led the way into the kitchen and breathed deep. Thank goodness, the place smelled of home cooking and brownies, not sickness and death.

"What are we looking for?" Christine asked.

"Evidence," Nicki said. "Some sort of clue to show us what she wants. Did she like peaches as a kid? I don't know where we could get any real peaches in November, but maybe if we brought a bowl of plastic peaches she'd be happy enough to do her exercises and get well."

"Peaches could have been the name of a favorite pet or stuffed animal," Laura said. "I had a plush bunny named Snowball once. I carried him around for years."

Meredith propped her elbow on the counter. "It's entirely possible that she is recalling something from her childhood. I read that our oldest memories are the hardest to lose. Memory is like one of those old vinyl records—the grooves that have worn the deepest through time contain the memories we'll keep."

"So let's look for photo albums, scrapbooks, letters, and storage trunks," Christine suggested. "I'll bet she saved everything. She likes old stuff."

Kim headed for the stairs. "I'll check her room for old toys, dolls, or animals."

"I'll go through the cards in the desk," Laura volunteered. "I want to know more about her romance with Alden."

"I'll go through the kitchen and garage," Meredith said. "If it's real peaches she's so crazy about, maybe she'll have some canned peaches set aside somewhere."

Nicki looked at Christine. "Well, I guess you and I will cover the rest of the house. Let's start at the front door and work our way forward."

Six

The five girls searched for an hour, then gathered around the kitchen table to compare notes.

"That old garage is loaded with the usual stuff," Meredith reported. "Old bikes, bedsprings, tools, and paint cans. But on one shelf I did find this." She pulled a quart-sized Mason jar from her lap and set it on the table. Nicki could see something brown inside.

Christine made a face. "Could those be peaches? And do you think she canned them herself?"

"If they are, I wouldn't want to eat them now," Meredith said, grinning. "The label says 'M.A.'s favorite peaches—June 1987.'"

Nicki made a face. "Those peaches are older than we are."

"But M.A. must be Mary Alice," Kim said. "Perhaps it was Mary Alice who liked peaches so much."

Nicki nodded. "And when Mary Alice died, Mrs. Greaves couldn't stand the thought of eating her daughter's favorite peaches . . . so they've been sitting out there in the garage since 1987."

"There are other jars out there, too," Meredith said. "Green beans, jelly, corn, and all kinds of jam and tomato sauce. Most of it is pretty old."

"Maybe she left that stuff out there because she doesn't like going out to the garage," Christine pointed out. "After all, she's eighty years old and she probably doesn't like bugs and rats and roaches—garages are full of those kinds of things. Plus, to even get to the garage she'd have to climb up and down the back porch steps, and that could be dangerous for an old person."

Meredith agreed. "The garage is really dirty, which surprised me, because Mrs. Greaves is a good housekeeper. But it looks like she hasn't stepped foot in her garage in at least ten years."

Christine crinkled her nose. "So why would she ask for a jar of eighteen-year-old peaches? That doesn't make sense."

"Nothing makes sense if you've lost part of your memory," Meredith pointed out. "Maybe in Mrs. Greaves's mind, it's 1987 now and she's thinking of Mary Alice and Robert and those peaches. Anyway, it's worth a try, isn't it? Let's take them to the hospital and show them to her."

"Just don't feed them to her," Christine warned. "We should probably label that jar with a skull and crossbones."

Nicki smiled. "We will—*after* we show them to her."

"I have something to show, too," Kim said. She pulled a doll from her lap. "In the first bedroom, on the bed, I found this old doll."

Christine ran her fingertip over the doll's delicate porcelain face. "Wow. That doll is *old!*"

Kim nodded. "You will notice the doll is wearing a faded dress that is the peach-colored," Kim said, "and look at this." She lifted the mussed dark hair of the doll and exposed its delicate neck. There, on the white china surface, a childish hand had written Peaches.

Christine flashed a wide grin. "That must be it!" she said. "Peaches was her favorite childhood doll and this is Peaches!"

"That is not all." Kim quietly reached down and brought up another doll, this one just as old and worn, but with golden hair and wearing a faded blue dress. She turned the second doll over, lifted its hair, and held it up for the girls to see. The same childish hand had written on the neck of this doll, too: Lela.

Christine looked at Nicki. "That's Mrs. Greaves's first name, right? Why would she name a doll after herself?"

"Maybe she had two dolls and gave them her two favorite names," Laura suggested. "She named one Peaches and the other Lela. She was an only child, remember. She must have been lonely as a kid."

Nicki thought a moment, then smiled. "At least we found two good ideas. Tomorrow after school we'll go to the hospital and show Mrs. Greaves the jar of peaches and the doll. If they don't make her happy, well, there's still plenty of digging left to do here."

Laura sighed. "I haven't even made a dent in those things in the desk."

"And I haven't finished the foyer," Nicki said, remembering all the old pictures in the hallway. "And we still don't know anything about Mrs. Greaves's grandson except that his name is -"

"Howard," Christine said. "Horrible Howard who never visits his grandmother."

—

Nicki nearly gave up the plan of helping Mrs. Greaves the next afternoon. She was closing her locker and getting ready to meet the others when Scott Spence stepped into her path.

"Hi, Nicki."

Scott's smile always made Nicki feel a little weak in the knees. Every girl in school had a crush on Scott, and Nicki always reminded herself that she was Scott's friend, not one of the girls who got all giggly every time he walked by. But he was so cute and nice that Nicki couldn't help feeling a little wobbly whenever he stopped to talk to her.

"Hi, yourself." She smiled and slung her book bag over her arm. "How's your dog?"

Scott laughed, remembering, no doubt, how Nicki and her friends had helped clear up a mystery involving Scott's dog McArthur: The Case of the Mystery Mark. "Mack's fine."

Scott looked at the ground and Nicki could barely hear his next words: "Would you like to go to the concert in the park this afternoon? My brother's jazz band is playing and I'd like you to come along . . . if you want. Jazz is more fun, you know, when you've got someone to listen with you."

Nicki bit her lip as a wave of feelings crashed over her. First came giddy happiness—she'd love to go—but feelings of responsibility and disappointment followed that crash of joy.

"Oh man." She shook her head. "I'd love to go, Scott, I really would, but I can't. I've got to go to the hospital this afternoon."

Scott's eyes narrowed in concern. "Kim Park's mother is better, isn't she?" Scott had been one of the Pine Grove Middle School students who helped raise money for the Park family when Mrs. Park needed her kidney transplant.

"Mrs. Park is fine, it's Mrs. Greaves we're going to see. We met her a few weeks ago, and she had a stroke while we were at her house. We're trying to help clear up a little mystery so she can get better."

She smiled and tried to look as sad as she felt. "I'd love to go, really. But I can't."

Scott shrugged. "It's okay. I just thought you might like jazz." He backed away. "See you around, okay?"

Nicki felt a sudden urge to run after Scott and forget about her friends and Mrs. Greaves. She sighed. Was Meredith right? Were old people nothing but trouble?

This time the girls were brave enough to smile and wave at the stern charge nurse at the desk. She frowned as they walked by, but they were quiet and kept out of the way, so she didn't protest as they crept toward Mrs. Greaves's room.

Christine stepped into the room first, but stuck her head back into the hall after a minute. "There's no change," she said, her eyes sad. "She looked right at me and asked for peaches."

"Okay." Nicki looked at Meredith. "Take in the jar of peaches."

Meredith shoved the jar at Nicki. "You can take it in. I don't like old people and I really don't like seeing them in hospitals."

Nicki rolled her eyes, but she took the jar and followed Christine back into the room. "Hello, Mrs. G.," she called. "It's Nicki. I brought you some peaches."

Mrs. Greaves hadn't changed. Her hair, which had always been combed and wavy, lay close to her head. Her eyes, which had sparkled with life and energy, seemed focused on something in the distance the girls couldn't see.

"You made these peaches," Nicki said as she lifted the heavy jar. "Were these Mary Alice's favorite food?"

She held the jar in front of Mrs. Greaves's eyes, but the woman gave no response. She only raised her right brow and murmured again, "Peaches. I want Peaches."

Nicki leaned toward Christine. "She seems better. That was a complete sentence, at least."

"Yeah, but the canned peaches didn't do a thing for her," Christine whispered. "I'll go out and tell Kim to bring in the doll. Maybe that'll do the trick."

Kim came into the room and automatically bowed to the bedridden Mrs. Greaves. "Good afternoon," she said, lifting the doll from a shopping bag she'd found. "I believe this may be precious to you?"

When she held the doll so Mrs. Greaves could see it, for the first time the girls saw a glimmer of recognition in the woman's eyes. Mrs. Greaves's chin quivered and a tear slid out from beneath her drooping eyelid. But her response was the same: "Peaches. I want Peaches."

"I don't think Peaches is a doll," Nicki whispered. "She recognizes it, I think, but it's not what she wants. We have to go back and look around some more."

Kim placed the doll on the nightstand next to the bed. "We will be back," she promised, bowing again.

—

Two hours later, the girls stepped through Mrs. Greaves's kitchen door. "See there?" Meredith demanded as they moved inside. "The house even smells like old people now. Musty."

Christine snorted. "If it smells musty, it's because it's been shut up," she said, walking down the hall to the front door. "Let's throw up some windows and air this place out."

"We really do need to find Howard today," Nicki reminded them. "My dad said someone in her family needs to know she's sick. We should make finding Howard a priority over finding out what peaches means."

Laura moved toward the living room. "I should be able to come up with something from the cards in the desk."

"I think I'll work in the kitchen," Meredith said. "I've had enough of that dark and dirty garage."

"The kitchen?" Christine laughed. "What do you expect to find in the kitchen?"

Meredith bristled. "Some people keep important papers in kitchen drawers. My mother hides her valuables in the freezer."

Kim sent Meredith a puzzled look. "The freezer?"

"In an empty orange juice can," Meredith explained. "And while I'm in there, I can make some lemonade. We might get thirsty."

Kim headed toward the stairs. "I will continue to work in the bedrooms."

"I think I'll go upstairs to the nursery," Nicki said. "Mrs. G said she was born up there, didn't she?"

Christine lifted her hands. "What should I do?"

Nicki paused on the staircase landing. "Why don't you take down the pictures in the hall and see if any of them are labeled? Maybe you can find the name of a relative we need."

Each girl began to work, sorting through drawers, cabinets, trunks, closets, and boxes. What wasn't useful was examined and returned to its place.

Nicki discovered a new appreciation for Mrs. Greaves's housekeeping. If the woman hadn't been so clean and tidy, this would have been a dusty, dirty job.

An hour later they met in the kitchen. Over glasses of lemonade they compared notes.

"I think I've found our grandson." Laura pointed to a diagram of Mrs. Greaves's family tree. "All we need now is a phone book. If he's listed, we can call Howard ourselves."

Nicki peered at the diagram. "Who is he?"

"Well." Laura paused to sift through a pile of cards she had pulled from the secretary. "This is such a tragic, romantic story I don't know where to begin. Okay—Mrs. Greaves was born in this house on December 20, 1925. Her maiden name was Huff. I found a birth announcement for Lela Alice Huff—see?"

She held up a tiny card of a baby in a buggy. "Anyway, she grew up, but her parents died from some kind of disease a few months apart from each other in 1944. I found copies of their obituaries. Lela—I mean, Mrs. Greaves—came home from college to nurse them, remember? She was only nineteen and suddenly all alone in the world."

"But she inherited this house," Christine pointed out. "She was probably a very eligible young woman."

Laura's eyes shone. "This is where it gets romantic. I found an engagement party invitation. Lela Alice Huff was engaged to marry Thomas Patrick Davis on Christmas Eve in 1944, but it never happened. I found a simple handwritten wedding announcement saying that she married Alden Greaves on December 20th of that year!"

Meredith lifted a brow. "She ran away and got married on her birthday. Pretty spunky for an old lady!"

Nicki elbowed Meredith. "She wasn't an old lady then." She looked back at Laura. "So . . . she eloped?"

Laura nodded. "I found several cards that congratulated her on her engagement to Thomas Davis, but nothing to congratulate her on her marriage to Alden Greaves. I figure it happened like this: Someone was pressuring her to marry and marry quickly, and this Thomas Davis must have been settled or rich or something. By all rights, she should have married him, moved into his house, and sold this one. But instead she married Alden and they lived here. What does that tell you?"

Christine thumped the kitchen table. "Alden Greaves didn't have a house!"

Laura nodded. "Right! I think it's so romantic—she married for love, not money or security. And one year later, in January 1946, they had a daughter, Mary Alice Greaves. I found cards in the desk that congratulate Lela on the baby's birth, so apparently Pine Grove society forgave her for leaving Thomas Davis without a Christmas bride."

Kim clasped her hands together. "That is a beautiful story."

"If it's true," Meredith muttered. "Laura can romanticize things."

"It's logical," Nicki said. "So . . . what happened next?"

Laura consulted her notes. "From what I can tell, Alden died suddenly in 1953, when Mary Alice was seven. So Mrs. Greaves had to raise her daughter alone. The desk has hundreds of cards from Mary Alice to her mother, and in 1966, Mary Alice married Robert Simon." Laura flipped a page of notes. "Apparently they were married for some time without kids, but in 1970 they had a son, Howard Simon."

Meredith crinkled her brow. "So Howard is now thirty-five."

"Yep. I found lots of cards from Howard to his grandmother when he was small, but there's nothing in the desk from him in the last fifteen years."

Christine leaned forward and lowered her voice. "What happened to Mary Alice and Robert?"

Laura pressed her lips together. "I gotta warn you, this is sad." She pulled a faded newspaper column from her notebook, then held it up so they could read the headline: 'Couple Killed Saving Son and Friend.'

Christine took the clipping and read aloud:

Robert Simon, 43, and his wife, Mary Alice, 42, were killed at 1 AM Sunday morning when their car stalled on the railroad tracks south of U.S. Highway 29. Police estimate the couple had time to escape the oncoming train, but apparently turned to wake their 17-year-old son, Howard, and his friend, Daniel Smith, who were sleeping in the back seat. The couple was killed, but the boys were thrown clear of the wreckage and survived. The conductor of the train said he couldn't see the car in the darkness until it was too late to stop.

The family and their guest were returning from an overnight camping trip in nearby Achula Springs. "My parents stayed in the car to wake us up," a distraught Howard Simon told police investigators. "They saved my life."

"Oh man." Nicki wiped a tear from her eye. "In a minute, Mrs. Greaves lost everyone except her grandson."

"But the worst thing is that he might as well be dead, too," Laura said. "That desk is full of cards from friends of years past, church members, and so on, but there's nothing from Howard . . . unless she keeps his stuff separate for some reason."

Christine scratched her chin. "Maybe they had a fight and she threw his cards out."

"I doubt it," Laura answered. "She keeps everything."

Nicki stood. "At least we know his name now. I'll call information and see if he lives in the area. Howard Simon needs to know his grandmother is in the hospital."

A moment later Nicki had the number. She dialed it carefully and listened as the phone rang twice. A hoarse voice answered, "Hello?"

"Mr. Simon?"

"Who's this?"

"You don't know me, but I'm a friend of your grandmother's."

"If you want to nag me about visiting her, forget it. Did she tell you to call?"

"No, sir. I thought you should know she's in the hospital. She had a stroke."

The man fell silent, then Nicki heard him whisper, "Oh wow. Is she going to make it?"

"The doctors think so."

"Oh man."

Nicki paused. Was that relief or desperation in his voice? "My friends and I," she said, "are looking after her house and the dog while she's in the hospital, but if you want to take over—"

"I'm sure you've got it handled. If it looks like she's really bad off, call me again, will you?"

Nicki rolled her eyes. This guy was not at all like Mrs. Greaves—somehow the passing of generations had diluted the family charm. "If you want to see her, she's at Pine Grove Community Hospital."

"Got it." The phone clicked. Howard Simon had hung up.

A forgotten idea reoccurred to Nicki as she placed the telephone in its cradle. Was this the man who had screamed at Mrs. Greaves so many weeks ago? Whether it was or not, Horrible Howard was a definite creep.

Seven

Meredith was upset the next morning. "I can't go over to Mrs. Greaves's today," she told Nicki. "My mom insists that I go shopping with her. She even canceled her afternoon class at the university so we could shop together."

"Shopping?" Laura's head swiveled around. "I love to shop. What are you shopping for? New clothes? Shoes?"

Meredith moaned. "No such luck. We're shopping for her. She wants me to help her pick out—are you ready for this?—funky clothes, she said. My mother wants to look hip."

Christine gave Meredith a sympathetic smile. "That's too bad."

Nicki nodded. They had been so wrapped up in the search for Mrs. Greaves's family that they had nearly forgotten that Meredith was going through a rough time with her parents' divorce.

The bell rang and their homeroom teacher, Mrs. Balian, stood to take attendance. Meredith was still muttering about shopping with her mother, and Nicki had to smile at the thought. It was hard to imagine Meredith's mom, the mathematics professor, looking hip.

"Why is she doing this?" Laura whispered to Meredith. "I thought your mom was the suit and bun type." She paused. "Is it—do you think—could it be because of the divorce?"

Meredith shrugged. "Maybe. But she also found her first gray hair. That happened before they started talking about divorce."

"Try to have a good time this afternoon," Nicki said, turning sideways to look at her friends. "Christine is going to the hospital after school to stay with Mrs. Greaves. Laura, Kim, and I are going back to the house to keep looking for peaches. If you get back early, come on over."

Meredith sighed. "Okay. But this sounds like one of those all-afternoon mother-daughter things."

Nicki felt someone staring at her from across the room. She looked up and caught Scott's eye, but he turned his attention to the cover of his notebook.

Nicki bit her lip. She must have embarrassed him when she turned down his invitation to hear the jazz band. The last thing she ever wanted to do was hurt his feelings, but how could she tell him that without embarrassing him even worse?

At that moment, she had no answers.

That afternoon when they unlocked Mrs. Greaves's kitchen door, Nicki stepped inside and sniffed the air. "It smells better since we cracked the upstairs windows," she said, thinking of Meredith's comments. "There's no musty smell at all."

Buttons came skittering down the hall, yapping with excitement. Laura stepped over him and headed toward the living room, but Kim knelt to play with the lively dog. "Christine is at the hospital," Kim told Buttons, "but we will talk to you. Are you hungry?"

As Kim moved toward the pantry, Nicki tried to decide where she should begin her search for peaches. Had Meredith finished in the kitchen? She thought she'd take a quick look around before heading upstairs to help Kim look through the bedrooms and nursery. After that, there was always the attic.

Kim poured a bowlful of dog food and put the bag back into the pantry. As she shut the door, Nicki stopped her and pointed to the inside of the door. "Look! Do those scratches look strange to you?"

The door had been painted several times and was now a glossy white, but even through the paint Nicki could see horizontal lines scratched onto the edge of the door. The deep lines began about three feet from the floor and continued up the door until the last was even with Nicki's head.

She checked the door frame. There were no protruding nails or screws that could have caused the scratches.

"Do you know what this looks like?" she asked, her excitement rising. "Do your parents ever measure you and mark your height on the wall?"

Kim shook her head. "We live in an apartment. We cannot write on the wall."

"My parents have this one spot in our house where they measure us," Nicki said. "Every three or four months Mom makes us stand against the wall and Dad marks how tall we've grown."

Nicki studied the scratched surface. "My parents chose a spot behind the bathroom door—you know, so it wouldn't be real obvious. I'll bet someone in Mrs. Greaves's family used the back of this door to do the same thing."

Kim pointed to the scratches. "There are many marks. How do we know whose growth was recorded?"

Nicki ran her fingertips over the painted surface. She paused when she felt a rough spot at the top of the door. "Do you have a quarter in your purse?"

Kim pulled a quarter out of her wallet and handed it to Nicki. Nicki held her breath and used the edge of the quarter to scratch at the rough spot over the outermost row of marks. The top layer of paint scraped away easily, except for where it had settled into a pair of deeply carved initials: L.H.

"Lela Huff!" Kim's eyes shone with delight. "Mrs. Greaves's parents marked her growth here."

"Wow, I didn't realize she was as tall as I am," Nicki said. She grinned, finding it hard to imagine their elderly friend as a tall, thin girl. "I wonder if she got called 'beanpole,' too."

Kim pointed to another rough spot over a middle row of marks. Nicki scratched at the paint and a moment later, another pair of initials appeared: P.B.

Nicki looked at Kim. "Could that be Peaches? Was Peaches a person?"

Kim tapped at the third rough spot. "Quick, try this one."

The third set of initials made sense: M.A.G.

"Mary Alice Greaves," Nicki said, handing the quarter back to Kim. "Lela used the door to record her daughter's growth, too."

Kim ran her fingertips over the door. "Are there any dates?"

Nicki sighed. "I don't think so. And I don't think I ought to scratch the paint off the entire door to find out."

Kim pressed her hand to her forehead. "Wait—I remember something. Come with me to the nursery."

Nicki followed Kim upstairs. The nursery was a pretty room, splashed with sunshine from a wide window that overlooked Palm Avenue. The only furniture in the room now was an old dresser, but the room had obviously been designed for a child. The faded wallpaper featured scenes of two little girls at play—in one scene they were skipping rope, in another they were playing with jacks, in another they were picking flowers . . .

Kim pointed to a section of wallpaper. "Come and look."

Nicki looked at the place Kim indicated. Over the heads of the little girls, someone had scrawled "P.B. + L.H."

Nicki looked at her friend. "What are you thinking, Kim?"

Kim delicately touched the initials. "I think Peaches B. was Lela's best friend, her playmate." Kim's eyes softened. "They must have loved each other very much."

"That's possible," Nicki said. "Lela was an only child and she probably wanted someone to play with. If Peaches was a neighbor or a relative, they could have grown up together. Lela's parents marked their growth together on the pantry door."

Kim shook her head. "But how do we find out who she is?"

Nicki pointed to the stairs. "We'll see if Laura has found any clues in the old desk. If she hasn't, I have another idea . . ."

The clues in the wallpaper and on the back of the pantry door fascinated Laura, as Nicki had known they would. "Imagine, Peaches is a real person," Laura said, sighing happily.

"This is where you come in," Nicki said. "Have you seen any cards or papers about Peaches in the secretary? If she was Lela's best friend, surely there has to be something about her in all this stuff."

Laura shook her head. "I haven't seen anything at all. But maybe Peaches is a nickname."

"What about the initial B?" Kim asked. "Are there any cards from friends or family with a last name beginning with B?"

Laura frowned as she wrapped a strand of hair around her fingers. "There might be. So far I've been looking for Peaches, Mary Alice, Alden, Robert, or Howard. Everything else I've tossed into one big pile."

"Maybe you should go back through that pile," Nicki suggested. "In the meantime, I'm going to call my mom and ask about the house next door. If Peaches was a neighbor, she either lived next door or down the street. On this corner lot with the river across the road, the Huffs didn't have too many neighbors."

Kim gave her a puzzled look. "Why will your mother know about the house?"

"Real estate agents know how to trace the backgrounds of houses," Nicki explained. "Everything about the owners is recorded down at the courthouse. Well, not everything. But you'd be surprised what you can learn."

Nicki called her mother, explained the problem, and hung up. "It'll take a while," she told the other girls when they met in the kitchen, "but we might learn something."

Suddenly Buttons leapt from his gingham bed and began to growl. He moved toward the front door, his tail stiff and his eyes bright.

Laura edged away. "He isn't going to bite, is he?"

Nicki heard steps across the front porch, followed by the sound of a key in the lock.

"Uh-oh," she whispered. "Someone's coming in."

Eight

Snarling and snapping, Buttons flew toward the door like a terrier-sized terror.

Nicki motioned for Kim and Laura to sit at the table while she peered down the hall. Through the lace curtain that covered the window in the door, she could see the outline of a husky, masculine shape.

The lock clicked; the stranger opened the door. "Outta my way, mutt," the man said, kicking at Buttons. He missed, but Buttons didn't let up, remaining on full alert as the stranger stepped into the foyer.

Nicki didn't know who he was or what he intended, but she thought she'd better make her presence known. She took a deep breath and stepped into the hallway.

"Hello," she called with more confidence than she felt. "Can I help you?"

The solid man had the dark, wavy hair she remembered from the afternoon the stranger had yelled at Mrs. Greaves. His ordinary face wasn't particularly handsome, but that may have been because his features were screwed up in a scowl. "Who are you and what are you doing in my grandmother's house?"

Nicki took a half-step back. "You must be Howard Simon."

"I know who I am; who are you?" he asked again, then he remembered. "Are you one of those kids looking after the dog?"

Nicki nodded and snapped her fingers at Buttons, who was still growing. "Calm down, boy, it's okay."

"If you've fed him, you can be on your way, then." Howard gave her a stiff smile. "I'm going to check on the house. You haven't been messing around with things, have you?"

Horrible Howard strode past Nicki on his way to the kitchen.

"We haven't hurt anything," she said, lifting her chin. "Our parents know what we're doing and Mrs. Greaves trusts us."

"We'll see about that." He stopped in the kitchen doorway and blinked at the sight of Kim and Laura at the table. "More of you? Great day, how many kids have been inside this house? What sort of parties are you having in this place?"

"We're not having parties," Nicki said. "We're trying to help Mrs. Greaves."

Ignoring her, Howard moved to the cupboard. He took down a glass, then opened the fridge and peered inside. "Lemonade. Is that all she has to drink?"

"Your grandmother keeps asking for Peaches," Nicki said. "We are trying to find her. The doctor says she'll get better faster if she has what she wants, and the only thing she asks for is Peaches . . ."

Howard leaned against the kitchen counter and snorted. "You're wasting your time. I've heard all about Peaches—she was some imaginary friend my grandmother had when she was a kid. There is no Peaches, not in real life, anyway. She's a phantom."

"I think she was real." Nicki opened the pantry door and

pointed to the scratches. "See these marks? Her parents made growth marks for both Lela and Peaches."

Howard rolled his eyes. "They were just going along with the game," he said. "Haven't your parents ever humored you? I think your parents must humor you girls a lot."

As he moved toward them, the girls scattered out of his way like sheep avoiding a sheepdog. "Peaches was an imaginary playmate and she doesn't exist. Never did. Now, you girls go on home and leave my grandmother alone. Now that I know she's sick, I'll take care of everything."

Nicki was surprised when Kim, usually so quiet, stepped in Horrible Howard's path and looked directly into his eyes. "Have you seen her?"

Howard stared at her. "Have I what?"

"You heard me. Have you been to see her?"

"Of course," Howard answered. "Now, get your stuff together and get out of here."

The girls gathered their things and headed toward the back door. Nicki was about to step onto the back porch when the phone rang. "It's for me," she said to Howard as she ran into the hall. The man scowled again, but he didn't stop her from answering.

"Hello?"

Nicki listened, then smiled. "Okay. Thanks, Mom. I'm on my way home."

—

Once they had passed through the back hedge, Nicki turned to

Laura and Kim. "Peaches Brooke," she said, grinning. "The family that lived next door from 1925 until 1941 was named Brooke. Peaches *wasn't* just an imaginary friend."

Laura stopped in midstride. "That name rings a bell. I'm sure there were cards or something from a family named Brooke. Birthday cards, I think."

"You can check tomorrow when we go back to feed Buttons." Nicki felt ready to dance with excitement "I can't wait to tell Christine!"

"What about Howard Simon?" Kim interrupted. "I don't think he likes us at all."

Laura shrugged. "It doesn't matter what Mr. Simon thinks. Mrs. Greaves invited us to her house and asked us to look after her dog. Howard has nothing to do with our friendship with Mrs. Greaves."

"All the same, I know he doesn't want us around," Nicki said. "Something tells me we should steer clear of him as much as possible."

—

In homeroom the next morning, Laura, Kim, and Nicki told Christine and Meredith the latest news. "Peaches was probably Peaches Brooke, the next-door neighbor," Nicki explained. "But her family sold the house in 1941."

Meredith thought a moment. "Lela would have been sixteen and away at school that year. Perhaps that's when the girls lost touch with each other."

"And when Lela came home to nurse her sick parents, she didn't have time for socializing," Christine said. "She only had time for her parents—"

"—and Alden Greaves," Laura said. "She was all caught up in responsibility and love."

Meredith lifted a warning finger. "Pearl Harbor was attacked in 1941, too, so the world was at war. Adulthood must have seemed awfully frightening for a young girl faced with so much."

"Peaches must have slipped her mind," Kim said.

The morning bell rang and the class quieted while Mrs. Balian checked the roll and the morning announcements thundered from the intercom.

"How was Mrs. Greaves yesterday?" Kim asked Christine when the announcements were over.

Christine shook her head. "She seemed a little better, but she kept insisting she wanted Peaches. Now she's saying it more forcefully, though, so I think she is getting stronger." She paused. "But the one thing that really breaks my heart is that I was her only visitor. The nurses let me go right in because they said no one has visited her at all."

Nicki stared at Chris. "No one? But Howard said he'd been to see her."

"He was lying," Christine answered. "Unless he's the invisible man."

"Well, as much as I hate hospitals and old people, I'd rather go there today than shopping with my mother again," Meredith said.

Laura laughed. "Didn't you have a good time?"

"No way. My mom's on some kind of weird kick. First she had all her hair chopped off so now it's shorter than my dad's. Then we went out to dinner and she embarrassed me to death—I think she was flirting with the waiter. Honestly, I wanted to crawl under the table and die."

Christine giggled.

"Not funny," Meredith said. "Then she bought a copy of *Style* magazine and picked out three outfits she liked. She went into all the stores, pointed to the magazine and said, 'Do you have something like this?' They'd say yes and pull out something in my size, but then Mom would say, 'No, it's for me.'" Meredith shuddered dramatically. "It was absolutely the most humiliating day of my life."

Nicki's gaze drifted to the other side of the room, where Corrin Burns and Michelle Vander Hagen were flirting with Scott Spence. If Scott had been embarrassed or hurt yesterday, he was certainly making up for it today. Scott knew that Corrin and Michelle weren't exactly Nicki's best friends.

"Okay, Scott," Nicki whispered, "if our friendship ends over this, it ends. I'm leaving it all up to you."

Nine

After school that afternoon, Laura stepped through the back door and headed straight toward Mrs. Greaves's old secretary. "I'll look for cards that say Brooke," she told the others. "I know I'll find something today."

Kim had volunteered to go to the hospital to sit with Mrs. Greaves, and Christine was eager to search in the house. "Why don't we tackle the attic today?" she asked Nicki. "Maybe we can find some old letters or yearbooks or something to let us know what happened to Peaches."

Nicki agreed, so she, Christine, and Meredith climbed the staircase to the second floor, then looked at the rectangular opening in the ceiling. "It's a pull-down ladder," Meredith said. "You pull on that hanging cord and half of the ladder comes down. We'll have to slide the rest of the ladder down ourselves."

Nicki caught the rope and gave it a tug. The hinges on the attic door squeaked in protest, but the trapdoor opened halfway. Nicki could see the ladder.

"Pull harder!" Meredith said. "Here, let me help."

Together they pulled until the ladder was fully extended. Meredith climbed up about five steps and looked around.

"Is it dark up there?" Nicki asked.

Christine peeked out from behind her fingers. "Do you see any bats?"

"Nope, it's not dark because there's a window," Meredith said.

66

"And no, I don't see any creepy-crawly things. Come on up."

They all climbed up the ladder.

"Wow," Christine said, looking around. The attic was crowded with trunks and boxes that overflowed with old dresses, dishes, books, and trinkets. Lampshades hung from nails in the eaves, three dingy Easter baskets sat on the windowsill, and a strand of Christmas lights dangled from a makeshift shelf in the corner. The place had the musty, mysterious smell of age.

"Incredible." Meredith lifted the lid of an old trunk and pulled out a delicate lace dress. "A lot of this stuff is valuable. It's like a museum up here."

Nicki walked over to the window. "What a view! You can see miles of the river and most of River Road. Those boats down there look like toys."

Meredith stepped up and looked over Nicki's shoulder. "So does that car—uh-oh. Why is that car stopping here?"

Nicki groaned as a dark-haired man got out. "It's Horrible Howard. We'd better get out of here."

"Who?" Christine asked.

"I forgot, you haven't met the grandson," Nicki said, stepping over boxes. "Believe me, you don't want to."

The girls hurried down the ladder, pushed it back into place, and scurried down the stairs. Through the window of the front door they could see Howard Simon and another man on the front lawn. Howard was pointing at the windows and saying something about the house.

"Quick, into the living room!" Nicki whispered.

As Howard's footsteps lumbered across the wooden front porch, the girls darted across the hall and slipped into the living room. Laura looked up from the secretary. "What's happening?"

Nicki pressed her finger across her lips and pointed to the front door.

At that moment the front door opened. Howard stepped in and turned, and in that instant Nicki knew they'd been spotted.

Well, it wasn't like they were doing anything wrong.

Howard turned to the man with him. "Why don't you wait on the porch for a moment, Mr. Phillips," he said, his voice as smooth as butter. "I need a minute."

He closed the door, then stepped into the living room. "How long does it take you girls to come in and feed the dog?" he asked, lifting a brow. "Perhaps you should give me your key so I can take care of the dog myself. I don't want you hanging around my grandmother's house."

"We're not hanging around," Nicki explained. "We discovered that Peaches was a real person. Her name was Peaches Brooke and her family lived next door until 1941. She wasn't a phantom friend at all, so we're still trying to find her."

"So why are you here?" Howard asked. "Surely you don't think she's buried under the floorboards. Or maybe you think she's locked away in a secret room in the attic? Is that what you think?"

Now he was making fun of them. Nicki pressed her lips together and didn't reply.

Laura cleared her throat. "Um, I found something that y'all should see." She held up a small white card. "In this card, someone wrote that Priscilla Brooke died of pneumonia in 1931. Could Priscilla be another name for Peaches Brooke?"

Howard sighed heavily. "I'm sure of it. In her mind, Grandmother has gone back to her childhood and she can't remember that her friend died. If you girls keep bringing this Peaches thing up, you're only going to upset her." He cleared his throat and looked Nicki in the eye. "I won't have you upsetting her. Am I making myself clear?"

Without waiting for an answer, Howard stepped into the living room and sat on the sofa, then patted the cushions. "I think you girls ought to know that I did call Grandmother's doctor today. He says she isn't improving, so I'm going to have her discharged and move her in with me. I can hire a private day nurse while I'm working, and she will be living with family. I think that's the best thing for her, don't you agree?"

Nicki looked at Laura. In any other case it might be a good idea, but she wouldn't send her worst enemy to live with Horrible Howard.

"Will you be able to spend time with her?" Nicki asked.

"Lots of time," Howard answered, smiling. "I'm a private investor, so I have a flexible schedule."

Christine looked at Nicki. "Mrs. Greaves did get awfully lonely living here by herself."

"This way she won't be lonely at all," Howard said. "Plus, since she's had a stroke, there's no way she can keep up with this big house. I'm going to close it up until . . . well, until she gets better."

Meredith pointed to the dog. "What about Buttons?"

"I guess the dog will have to move in with me, too." Howard smiled. "So you girls can run on along."

Nicki shook her head. "But—"

"Run along now." Howard's smile vanished. He stood and moved toward the phone. "You wouldn't want me to call the police, would you?"

Laura stood, her face pale. Nicki, Meredith, and Christine grabbed their book bags and joined Laura in moving toward the back door.

"The police!" Laura hissed as they left. "I've never had anyone threaten me with the police!"

Nicki let the back door slam, then settled her book bag on her back. "Don't worry—we have Mrs. Greaves's permission to visit her house. But I don't want to get in Horrible Howard's way. He's up to something, I know it."

Meredith frowned. "How can you tell?"

Nicki shrugged. "I don't know. Something about him just doesn't feel right."

Ten

The girls walked to Meredith's father's apartment where Laura phoned for a ride home. Meredith sat on a barstool at the kitchen counter, her forehead crinkled in thought.

"What's wrong?" Christine asked, leaning on the counter. "Are you thinking about your parents again?"

Meredith shook her head. "Something's not right. Laura, tell me again what you read on that little card."

Laura shrugged. "It said Priscilla G. Brooke, 1925–1931, died of pneumonia."

Meredith grinned. "Okay—if Priscilla was Peaches, she died when she was six, right?"

Nicki did the math in her head. "Right."

"But the growth marks in the pantry showed that the girls were tall, didn't they?"

Nicki gasped. "Yeah—Lela was as tall as me, and Peaches' last mark was only about two inches shorter."

"How many over five-feet-tall six-year-old girls do you know?" Meredith smiled.

Christine clapped. "Peaches didn't die! Peaches is *not* Priscilla!"

Nicki grinned. "Unless they measured a ghost."

"If Peaches isn't Priscilla, who is she?" Meredith asked. "Laura, did you find anything else in the secretary that might help us?"

Laura blushed. "Maybe. I was going through all the cards, sorting all the Brooke notes in a pile. When Howard came in I stuck the whole pile in my notebook. I didn't mean to take them out of the house, but"—she pulled her notebook from her book bag—"here they are."

Laura spread a stack of cards on the kitchen table.

"You can return them tomorrow," Nicki said. "But let's see what you've got."

Christine pulled a card from the stack. "Happy birthday to Lela from the Brooke family," she read. "Here's another—Happy Valentine's Day from P. Brooke."

"That could be from Peaches or Priscilla," Meredith said, bringing a tray of sodas to the kitchen table.

"Here's a Christmas card." Nicki pulled a colorful card from the stack and felt her heart thump when she saw the signature. "Wow—it's from the entire Brooke family. It's signed from David, Ruby, Eunice, Floyd, and Priscilla Brooke."

"Big family," Christine said. "Just like mine. We started having our Christmas cards imprinted. Saved my mom from writer's cramp."

Nicki ran her finger over the names on the card. "If David and Ruby are the parents, then Eunice, Floyd, and Priscilla must be the children."

Meredith picked up her thought. "And since Priscilla couldn't have been Peaches and Floyd probably wasn't Peaches, then Peaches must be—"

"Eunice?" Laura made a face. "Why would you call someone named Eunice 'Peaches'?"

Christine grinned. "Who knows? Maybe she liked to eat peaches."

"We may never know why," Nicki said, "but the important thing is to find her. We know that Priscilla is dead, and our only chance to help Mrs. Greaves is to find Eunice and see if she is Peaches. Let's look for letters, a yearbook, or a scrapbook. Probably only her family and Lela called her by her nickname."

"To get back in the house we're going to have to get past Horrible Howard," Meredith said. "What do you suppose he was doing there today? And who was that other man?"

Nicki shook her head. "Something tells me Mrs. Greaves wouldn't be happy living at Howard's place."

The girls looked up as Mr. Dixon entered, pushing the bike he rode to his job as an English professor at the university. He grinned when he saw the girls crowded around his kitchen table.

"Hello, girls," he said. "What brings you all here? Don't tell me they've closed the malls and you have nowhere else to hang out."

Nicki grinned. "We were at Mrs. Greaves's house and her grandson asked us to leave."

Laura lifted her chin. "He said he'd call the police on us. Can you believe it?"

Mr. Dixon took off the cap he always wore when riding his bike. "Sounds like you girls are on the verge of being involved in a family squabble." He unhooked his satchel from the bike. "I'd avoid trouble if I were you. There's nothing worse than the old and the young in a family at war with each other."

"They're not at war," Meredith explained. "Howard wants his

grandmother to come live with him as soon as she can leave the hospital. He's mad at us for something."

Mr. Dixon nodded. "Probably for interfering."

"But we're not interfering," Nicki said. "We're only trying to help Mrs. Greaves get better."

"One of us visits her every day in the hospital," Laura pointed out. "That's more than Howard does."

"Then he shouldn't mind your help," Mr. Dixon said, "unless he thinks you're in his way."

"I don't know how we could be in his way," Laura said. "We all want Mrs. Greaves to get better."

"The old and the young frequently don't understand each other." Mr. Dixon opened a book he'd pulled from his satchel. "Listen to this proverb: The glory of young men is their strength, gray hair the splendor of the old."

Laura looked at him. "What does that mean?"

Nicki spoke up. "Young men have strength and older people have wisdom. Right, Mr. Dixon?"

He nodded.

Meredith crinkled her nose. "I never thought of old age as being wonderful. I've always thought of it as an incurable disease. Your body wears down, your cells wear out"—she grabbed her throat and made dramatic gasping sounds—"and then you die."

"Ah, every man desires to live long, but no man would be old," Mr. Dixon said. "Or at least that's what Jonathan Swift thought." The laugh lines around his eyes crinkled as he looked at his daughter. "It's a truly wise person who can see the beauty in old age, Meredith."

She shook her head. "I just don't see it."

The delicate three-note horn of the Cushmans' limo broke into the silence. "That's our ride," Laura said, gathering the cards on the table. "Come on, we'd better get moving."

Christine and Nicki gathered their things, but Meredith paused a moment. "Well, Dad, I've got to be going, too. Mom'll be waiting."

Mr. Dixon nodded. "I know. I'll see you this weekend." He smiled. "How is your mother, by the way?"

Meredith shrugged. "She's gone off the deep end. She's acting like a kid."

"Be patient with her, sweetheart. And tell her to read Shakespeare's Sonnet II."

Meredith frowned. "Why?"

"Never mind." He grinned as Laura's chauffeur tapped the car horn again. "You'd better get going."

—

"Well," Meredith told the girls the next afternoon at lunch, "my mother read Shakespeare's Sonnet II, just as Dad suggested. And I don't think it helped much."

"What is the second sonnet?" Laura asked.

Meredith pulled a thin volume of poetry from her book bag and began to read: "When forty winters shall besiege thy brow and dig deep trenches in thy beauty's field—"

Christine cackled. "I never did get poetry, but that doesn't sound very romantic."

"I get it," Nicki said. "The deep trenches are wrinkles. After forty years, the lady has wrinkles."

"That's the idea," Meredith said, closing the book. "Anyway, the point of the poem is that as people get older and their beauty fades, they should find joy in their children. Somehow, though, my mother didn't find that poem very comforting."

Laura sniffed. "I don't think I would, either. When I'm forty I might have a few laugh lines, but trenches? Shakespeare didn't know much about complimenting women."

"You're right." Meredith shrugged. "My mother didn't feel at all complimented."

Nicki looked around the circle at her friends. "I wonder . . . do you think Mrs. Greaves is proud of her grandson?"

Christine blinked. "What makes you ask that?"

"I don't know, just wondering."

"Well," Chris said, "maybe. He is going to move her in with him and get her a nurse. He's even going to take care of Buttons."

"She might get better living with Howard," Laura said. "Doesn't time heal everything?"

"Not if you're running out of time," Nicki said, remembering Mrs. Greaves's life expectancy chart.

Christine shook her head. "We have to trust Howard. He's her grandson, after all, and he can get her a nurse and take care of her. That's more than we could ever do."

Kim raised an eyebrow. "We will see," she said simply.

Eleven

The girls were walking out of the school's big double doors when Meredith recognized the familiar beep of her mother's Honda. "Wait, it's my mom," Meredith said, pointing to the tan SUV. "She probably wants to take us shopping."

The girls walked over and Meredith leaned toward the passenger's window. "What's up, Mom?"

Mrs. Dixon pointed to the back door. Nicki noticed she was wearing a leotard and Reeboks. "Hop in," she said. "I know I can't get Meredith unless I get you all, so I want you all to come with me to the gym." She snapped her gum and nodded. "I promise to have you all home by dinnertime."

Meredith's eyes widened in panic. "But Mom, we had plans to go see Mrs. Greaves in the hospital, plus we have to check on her dog," Meredith said. "We hadn't planned on going to the gym."

Mrs. Dixon looked thoughtful. "Okay, I'll be honest. Meredith, honey, I'm terrified of going to the gym alone. This will be my first time and I'm afraid I'll look like a fool."

Nicki, Laura, Christine, and Kim shifted their book bags as they stood and waited. Mrs. Dixon leaned toward them, her eyes pleading. "Won't you come with me this one time? I'll give you girls some money and you can get a drink at the juice bar while I take my exercise class. Then I'll drop you off at the hospital."

Meredith sighed, then turned to face the others. "Want a juice

77

break before we go to the hospital?" she asked, her voice heavy. "It'll save us walking a couple of miles."

The others nodded. "It's okay," Nicki said, opening the car door. "Who knows? Might be fun."

Mrs. Dixon chattered the entire way to the gym. "All the girls in my college classes swear by this new program," she said, "and I'm going to fight middle-age spread if it's the last thing I do."

"You look fine, Mom," Meredith said, her voice flat.

Mrs. Dixon flashed a smile in the rearview mirror. "Thanks, hon. But I'd expect you to say that."

She turned the car into a parking lot where a sign said "Tight and Trim, the Ladies' Gym."

Mrs. Dixon turned off the ignition and unbuckled her seat belt. "It took me an hour to find a gym for women only. No way on earth could I do this in front of a bunch of strange men." She turned and caught Nicki's eye. "Don't ever get old, girls. It's too much work."

Inside the gym, a Tight and Trim instructor met Mrs. Dixon at the door. "Harriet, so nice to see you," the girl chirped. "Are these your sisters?"

Meredith rolled her eyes as Mrs. Dixon giggled. "We're going to the juice bar, Mom," she called. "Pick us up when you're ten years younger."

Mrs. Dixon kept her promise and drove the girls to the hospital when her class was done. "I think I'll park here and take a nap," she mumbled as the girls climbed out. "Every bone aches and I think I pulled something back there in the gym. You girls go on and take your time. If I'm nearly dead when you come back, well, you won't have far to take me, will you?"

Meredith laughed and waved good-bye. "You'll survive, Mom. You're just out of shape."

The duty nurse was away from her desk, so all five girls tiptoed into Mrs. Greaves's room. Meredith was going to wait in the hall, but Nicki grabbed her arm and pulled her forward.

Mrs. Greaves was awake and, as usual, looking out the window. Kim spoke first. "Mrs. Greaves," she called, bowing, "we've come to see you again."

Mrs. Greaves turned her head. The side of her mouth twitched slightly.

"How are you?" Christine said, walking around to the side of the bed. "Buttons is fine, but he misses you. We've been taking good care of him."

Mrs. Greaves's mouth twitched again. Was she trying to smile?

"Peaches," she finally whispered. "I'd like to see Peaches."

Nicki elbowed Christine. "That's progress. That's the clearest sentence yet."

Kim bowed again. "We would like to find Miss Eunice Brooke, but we don't know how. Do you know where we could find her?"

Mrs. Greaves's eyes brimmed with tears. "Peaches," she whispered. "Eunice. She is my best friend."

Laura and Nicki gave each other high-fives. Christine took

Mrs. Greaves's hand and patted it gently. "Where is Eunice? Did she get married? Did she move away from Pine Grove?"

Mrs. Greaves seemed startled. "Of course not," she replied, her uncooperative muscles slurring her words slightly. "She's only a child. We're going to play in the attic."

Nicki felt her hope shrivel like a popped balloon. Now Mrs. Greaves wasn't making any sense at all.

She moved to stand next to Christine. "The doctor says you need to do your exercises so you can get better," she said. "Can we help you do them?"

Mrs. Greaves seemed to stare past Nicki. "Peaches is my best friend," she repeated. "I want Peaches." Her eyes filled with tears and a spasm contorted her face.

"We'd better go," Meredith said, tugging at Nicki's sleeve. "We might make things worse if we stay."

"Okay," Nicki said, stepping away. "But I want the nurse to make sure she's all right." She pressed the call button near the bedstand and picked up the old doll they had left there earlier. Mrs. Greaves had closed her eyes, but Nicki lifted the woman's good hand and placed the doll under it.

"Until we find Peaches," she whispered, "this will have to do."

Mrs. Greaves did not look down, but her arthritic fingers closed gently around the doll.

—

Meredith's mother seemed better by the time the girls returned to the car. "I'm fine," she said, smiling. "Got my wind back."

Christine laughed as she slid across the seat. "Just wait until tomorrow. You won't be able to move. My mom is always stiff the morning after she starts a new exercise program."

"Thanks, Christine, I needed to hear that." Mrs. Dixon waited until they were all in the car, then started the engine.

She dropped the girls at Mrs. Greaves's house and watched as they cut through the side yard and headed for the back door. "Meredith," she called, "don't stay too long. I'll have dinner ready at five."

Meredith waved her mother away. "Got it."

The girls trooped up the stairs. Christine turned Mrs. Greaves's skeleton key and opened the door. The girls gasped. The house was completely empty!

Twelve

Mrs. Greaves's house, which had been bursting with furniture, knickknacks, pictures on the wall, and rugs on the floor, was bare to the bone. The kitchen table was missing, as was the hall runner, the flowers on the kitchen windowsill, and the gingham dog bed. The living room had been stripped of all its beautiful old furniture, and the antique secretary, with its treasure trove of history, had vanished.

Christine's footsteps echoed through the empty hall as she ran to the front of the house. "What happened? Where's Buttons?"

"Gone," Nicki said, shivering.

"This is spooky." Meredith's voice bounced off the high ceilings and walls. "How could someone come in here and take everything?"

Laura moaned. "It's a tragedy! All the history in that secretary, all the antiques that have stood in this room for over a hundred years—it's a certified shame! Who could have done such a thing!"

Nicki was afraid she knew. "Meredith," she said, "you and Kim check out the garage and see if it has been cleaned out, too. Laura, will you and Christine give me a hand upstairs? Let's see if the entire house has really been swept clean."

Nicki, Laura, and Christine ran upstairs. All that remained in Mrs. Greaves's bedroom were the clothes in her closet. Her dresser was gone and the stockings, underwear, and nightgowns she had kept in it had been carelessly piled on the wooden floor.

"There wasn't much in the nursery to begin with, but everything's gone," Kim reported.

"The spare room's been emptied, too," Christine said. "Even the baby pictures she had on the wall in there are gone."

Nicki walked back to the hallway. "Let's check the attic. You'll have to give me a hand with this pull-down ladder." The retractable ladder came down more easily this time, and when Nicki climbed into the attic she could see that everything had been cleared out, even the dusty lampshades and the faded Easter baskets. "I don't believe it," she said, groaning. "This place was bursting with stuff yesterday and now there's nothing."

"Not even a dust bunny," Christine said, sinking to a step. "Somebody literally came in here and swept this place clean."

Nicki slid down the wall and sat on the plank floor. "Now we don't have anything to help us in our search. I just knew we were going to find some record of Eunice Brooke in all the stuff up here."

"Hey, Nicki," Meredith and Kim called from downstairs. "Where are you?"

"We're in the attic," Christine answered. "Come on up."

Meredith blinked at the attic's empty space. "Wow. I can't believe they cleared this place out in less than twenty-four hours. Someone had to bring in a professional moving crew to do this."

Laura's eyes flashed. "I think you're right—and I think we all know who would do such a thing!"

"Horrible Howard?" Christine asked. "But he's her grandson!"

Meredith held up a finger. "He said he was moving her into his house, didn't he? If she wasn't living here, he could sell her stuff and say she didn't need it."

Christine looked like she was about to cry. "But she loved this house and everything in it. I know she wouldn't want to leave it unless she had to."

"That's the thing about old age," Meredith said. "When elderly people can't take care of themselves anymore, they have to move into a home or some kind of center. If they're sick, they can't take care of a house."

"But Mrs. Greaves is getting better," Nicki said. "And if we find Eunice Brooke, I think she'll get better even faster. Anyway, Howard had no right to sell her stuff without her permission. I can't imagine her giving him permission to get rid of all her things."

"In her condition, I don't think she *could* give him permission," Meredith pointed out. "But that's all Howard needs. Permission by default."

Kim had been quietly walking around the attic. Now she looked out the window. "If two little girls play up here, what do they do?" she asked. She blushed. "Most houses in Korea don't have attics."

Nicki shrugged. "I don't know. I guess you could play dress-up with all the old clothes in the trunks."

"You could play store with all the stuff that used to be up here," Laura added. "You know—one person is the customer and the other is the store clerk."

"I'll bet you played that a lot as a kid," Christine teased.

Laura grinned. "Shopping is still my favorite activity."

Meredith spoke up. "You could play hide-and-seek in an attic. You could hide behind trunks or in the corners of the eaves." She stepped over to the side of the house where the brick chimney hugged the inside wall. "Look—here you could flatten yourself against the wall. The way the bricks stick out, this would be a great hiding place."

Nicki walked to the chimney. The walls and roof of the attic were wooden. In fact, she could see the tips of the nails that held the shingles in place. But the brick surface of the chimney was unique. It was, she realized, the most interesting part of the room.

"It would be funny if—" Christine stopped. "No, I'm sure Lela and Peaches would never do anything like that."

"What?" Nicki asked.

Christine's eyes shone with mischief. "Well, a chimney's hollow, right? Once a bird flew down the chimney at my aunt's house and my brothers chased it all around and broke nearly everything in sight. We haven't been invited back since."

Meredith folded her arms. "What's your point?"

"Well," Christine said arching a brow, "if you took out a brick or two, you could drop stuff down the chimney and it would land in the living room."

Meredith laughed. "Why would you want to do that?"

Christine shrugged. "For fun. Maybe a stink bomb or a fake frog or a rubber snake or water. Use your imagination."

Nicki smiled. "That's pretty far out." But she walked by the chimney again, pressing each brick with her fingertips to see if any were loose.

"Where is this going to get us?" Meredith asked. "If there is a loose brick, what's it going to prove except that Eunice and Mrs. Greaves were as crazy as Christine?"

"Anything that will jog Mrs. Greaves's memory will help," Nicki answered, still testing bricks. Christine, Laura, and Kim joined in.

Laura giggled. "My mother won't believe what I've done today," she said. "I've watched the 'Tight and Trim' aerobics class and poked about a hundred old bricks to see if two little girls threw a rubber snake down a fireplace. If she could only see me now!"

Christine laughed, too. "It's a wild idea, but a good one," she said, crawling on the attic floor as she tested the bricks along the bottom of the chimney. "If we ever go to my aunt's again, I'm going to check out her attic! I could run the garden hose through the upstairs window and . . . whoa!"

One brick gave way when she applied her weight to it. Christine pitched forward, falling neatly into Meredith's lap.

Meredith rolled her eyes. "Don't you ever do anything calmly?"

"That's it!" Christine sputtered. "I found the loose brick!"

Nicki knelt. "That brick is too far near the edge to be over the hollow part of the chimney," she said. "It must be just an ordinary loose brick."

Christine pulled the brick completely out of its resting place. "Wait! There's something here behind it. Look." She put her hand into a small space and pulled out a small bundle of envelopes. The envelope on top was addressed to Miss Lela Huff.

"Wow." Nicki crossed her legs and spread the envelopes on the wooden floor. "We can read these letters and see if there's a clue about Eunice."

"Who could they be from?" Christine wondered, turning a letter over. "Alden?"

Nicki brushed dirt off her pants and scooped the letters into a pile. "Maybe. But the ink's so faded we're going to have to go downstairs to read them. Too dark up here."

Meredith spoke up. "Why would Lela hide letters up here? She kept everything else downstairs. And who was she hiding them from, herself?"

Nicki shrugged. "Maybe she put them here for old time's sake. After all, she and Peaches liked to play here. Or maybe she hid them years ago and forgot about them."

Downstairs, the phone began to ring. The girls looked at each other. "Let's get it," Meredith said, racing for the ladder. "It could be one of our parents."

Meredith jumped off the ladder and was the first to reach the ground floor. She answered the phone. "Hello?" As Christine came up behind her, Meredith shook her head. "No, Howard Simon isn't here, at least not yet."

She listened again. "Okay, what's the message? Shady Grove . . . opening now . . . government support. Okay, I'll tell him."

She hung up and turned to face the others.

Nicki read the bad news in Meredith's face. "What's that about?"

Meredith spoke carefully. "Someone from Shady Grove wanted Howard to know that there's an opening now. And if the patient has Medicaid, she would be completely covered because they are supported by the government."

Kim's eyes widened. "Oh no!"

"What's wrong?" Laura asked.

Kim was so flustered that it took her a moment to think of the English words. Finally, she was able to speak: "Shady Grove is a home for nursing. My mother went there for a week after her operation, but it was so bad we brought her home to recover in our care."

Nicki tried to calm Kim down. "You mean it's a nursing home?"

Kim nodded. "But it is not good. The people there, most of them are old, most are strapped to their beds. There are not many nurses, and the patients lie in dirt. Many are covered in bedsores. The government pays most of the costs, but it is not enough. I cried when I saw the place. It is a terrible way to treat those we should honor and respect."

Christine's eyes blazed. "That low-down, sneaky Horrible Howard! He isn't planning to move Mrs. Greaves to his home at all. He's planning to put her in Shady Grove, and he isn't even willing to pay a dime!"

"Hey, you guys," Meredith said, her voice tight, "if that lady on the phone is right, we'd better get out of here. Horrible Howard is supposed to be here at any minute."

Thirteen

"I can't believe Howard would put Mrs, Greaves in a nursing home," Nicki said.

"I can't believe he'd lie to us," Christine muttered. "My father says the worst thing a person can do is lie. You can't trust anyone who lies."

Laura spread her hands. "Maybe it's all a coincidence," she said, but her eyes were doubtful. "Maybe he was asking about nursing homes in case she needs more care than a nurse at home could give her."

Kim shook her head. "We couldn't afford to hire a private nurse, but we brought my mother home from Shady Grove as soon as we could," she said. "A nurse told me that my mother was lucky. Almost all the old people at Shady Grove stay there until they die."

Their thoughts were interrupted by the sound of a car door slamming in the driveway. "Quick, we've gotta go," Laura said. "He said he'd call the police."

"Hide these letters, Chris," Nicki said, dropping the letters into Christine's hands. "I'm not running. I want to talk to Howard Simon."

Meredith crossed her arms. "I want to talk to him, too. I want to give him a message."

The girls remained in the kitchen until they heard the front door open, then they filed into the hallway. Howard Simon looked up, then shook his head. "I thought I told you girls to stay away. I told you I'd take care of the dog."

"What have you done with the things in this house?" Nicki looked him straight in the eye. "Those things belonged to Mrs. Greaves."

Howard moved past her without answering.

"By the way, I took a message for you," Meredith said. "Shady Grove, where you won't have to pay a dime, has an opening today. But if you think you're going to put Mrs. Greaves in there, you're—"

"I know what I'm doing," Howard said, picking up the telephone. He dialed a number, then turned and grinned at Nicki. "Hello, Pine Grove Police? I'd like to report a break-in. There's a gang of middle school girls that have been using my elderly grandmother's house as a hangout. It's 616 River Road. Can you send someone over right away? The girls are here now and I don't think they're willing to leave."

He listened a minute more, and then hung up. "The police are on their way over."

Laura turned pale and grabbed Nicki's shoulder for support.

Howard grinned. "If you stay here, you'll be in big trouble. If you leave and never come back, we can forget about all of this."

Nicki looked at her friends. She had never meant for them to get in trouble with the police. They had only wanted to do a good deed for a friend, but as her mother often said, no good deed goes unpunished . . .

She lifted her chin. "We're leaving."

"Give me your key first," Howard demanded. "I don't ever want to see any of you again."

Christine slowly slipped the key and its chain over her head.

She held it a minute, then glared at Howard. "I promised to take care of Buttons. I gave Mrs. Greaves my word, so I'm not giving you this key until I know Buttons is okay."

"That dumb dog is safe at my place," Howard said, snatching the key and chain from Christine. "Now, join your friends and get out of my life. Don't ever bother my grandmother again, either."

Christine turned on her heel, but as she followed Nicki and the others to the back porch, she let the screen door slam.

—

"What do we do now?" Meredith asked, leading the way to her father's apartment. "He actually called the police. If we go back there, we could be arrested."

Christine's eyes were wet with tears of frustration. "But Mrs. Greaves gave us permission, for heaven's sake. I don't see how he can come in here and tell us what to do. Where was he when she needed emergency help?"

"But he is her grandson and right now she's not able to take care of herself," Nicki said. "He has legal authority, and that's more than we have."

Meredith unlocked the door of her dad's apartment. The girls trooped inside and collapsed in the living room. "I just don't trust that Howard," Laura said. "Isn't there something we can do to make people believe that Mrs. Greaves wouldn't want him to sell all her stuff?"

"He had the house cleaned out," Nicki said. "That proves that he's not planning to let her go back home."

"That's not good enough," Meredith said. "He could say he was only keeping her stuff in storage until she gets better or, well, until she dies. I don't know how we could find out where he took the stuff."

"He's trying to get her into that awful Shady Grove place," Kim said, shuddering.

"He can say she might need additional nursing care," Meredith pointed out. "Although he did tell us he was going to hire a nurse for her at his house."

"He took Buttons," Laura pointed out.

"Buttons is safe at his house." Meredith shrugged, then paused. "Or is he? Is Horrible Howard the type to keep a Pekignese?"

"He doesn't seem like the animal-loving type at all," Christine said, fuming. "People who like animals are usually nice."

Nicki looked at Christine. "Where would you take a dog if you had no real intention of keeping it?"

Christine snapped her fingers. "The dog pound! How dare he!"

Nicki stood and moved toward the phone. "Meredith, where's your phone book?"

Once she had looked up the number, Nicki dialed the Pine Grove Animal Shelter. "Hello? I'm looking for a little dog that may have been turned in. He's a brown and black Pekignese. He was wearing a blue collar and we haven't seen him since yesterday. He answers to the name of Buttons."

Nicki listened for a moment, nodded, then hung up.

Christine's face fell. "He's not there, is he?"

Nicki reached for her book bag. "Laura, can you call Mr. Peterson to drive us to the animal shelter? A brown Pekignese in a blue collar was brought in last night."

—

Buttons nearly turned himself inside out when the girls greeted him.

"I'll need thirteen dollars for you to reclaim him," the girl at the desk told Nicki. The girls dug in their book bags and came up with a total of twelve dollars and fifty cents.

Laura pulled out her charge card. "Do you take plastic?"

The girl at the desk laughed. "Sorry."

"He isn't even our dog," Christine said. "We're picking him up for his owner—she's in the hospital."

The girl looked at them, then grinned at Buttons. "Aw, go on and take him." She waved them away. "I'm glad someone claimed him."

Nicki scooped the little dog into her arms, then looked around the circle. "Okay . . . so who wants to take him home tonight?"

Laura bit her lip. "I don't think my mother would much like the idea. She's a little particular about our carpets."

Christine rubbed Buttons's head. "As much as I love him, my mother put a six-month ban on any new pets at our house. Right now we have six kids and thirty-two animals, if you count the gerbils and the baby cockatiels."

Meredith shook her head. "No way. This is not a good time at my mom's place."

Kim looked thoughtful. "My mother is still recuperating, so my parents are fussy. I will keep him, but he would have to stay outside or in the laundry room."

"Don't worry, I'll take him," Nicki said. "I'll keep him until Mrs. Greaves gets better. Our dog Stooge won't mind. Nothing upsets him."

The girls climbed into the limo, then Laura tapped on the glass that separated the girls from the driver. "Mr. Peterson, can you take us to Nicki's? We want to drop the dog off at her house."

The gray-haired chauffeur nodded. "Yes, Miss Laura."

Nicki gave her friends a grim smile. "Do you realize what this means? We've caught Howard Simon in another bald-faced lie. Can we trust anything he's told us?"

Fourteen

When they arrived at Nicki's house, she warned them to be quiet. "My mom and dad might be working in the office," she said, reminding the others that both her parents worked at home. "So head for the family room. We can close the door in there and we won't bother anyone."

Mrs. Holland looked up when Nicki and her friends walked quietly through the foyer. "Hi, girls," she said, smiling. "It's been a slow day, so come on in and make yourselves at home." She walked over and ran her fingers through Nicki's hair. "How are things at Mrs. Greaves's house, honey? Any progress on your latest mystery?"

Nicki sighed and pointed to the furry brown bundle in Christine's arms. "You wouldn't believe it. That's Buttons, Mrs. Greaves's dog. Do you mind if he stays with us until she is out of the hospital?"

Mrs. Holland made a face. "Wouldn't he be better off at home?"

"He can't go home—Horrible Howard stripped the house and took Buttons to the animal shelter. We found him, but there's no telling what Howard might do if he gets his hands on Buttons again."

Mrs. Holland patted the dog's silky hair. "Well, if old Stooge doesn't mind, I suppose it's okay if Buttons stays here for a while. How is Mrs. Greaves today?"

"She's better, but we think she'd improve a lot faster if we could find Peaches," Meredith said. "But we're getting closer. We know Peaches' real name was Eunice Brooke."

When the phone rang, Mrs. Holland moved into her office to answer it. "Excuse me, girls."

Nicki put a finger across her lips while Mrs. Holland spoke on the phone.

"Pine Grove Realty," Mrs. Holland said. "No, I'm sorry, but Mr. Thomas is out showing a property. Can I take a message? Um. You're interested in selling? That's great. Uh-huh. What's the address? Sure, got it—616 River Road. And the house is vacant."

Nicki peeked around the corner and saw her mother scribble on a pink message pad. "Thank you for calling, Mr. Simon. Good-bye."

Kim, who'd been listening as well, slapped her hand across her mouth. Christine gasped. Nicki stepped into the doorway to her mother's office. "Mr. Simon? Was that Howard Simon?"

Mrs. Holland looked at the note she had just written. "Yes, Howard Simon. Who is he?"

"He's the man who called the police on us!" Laura said.

"He's the man who put Buttons in prison!" Christine said.

"He's the man who is going to put Mrs. Greaves in a nursing home!" Kim said.

"He's the man who completely cleaned out Mrs. Greaves's house," Meredith said.

"And now he's the man who wants to sell Mrs. Greaves's house," Nicki added.

Mrs. Holland frowned. "This is serious. If your friend really is getting better, he has no right to make these decisions for her. I can't believe he would try to unless he's convinced he can talk her into moving somewhere else. Sometimes people can talk older people into all sorts of things."

"It is unfair," Kim said. "In my country, we stand up when older person enters the room. Our elders live with us and are respected. They are served first at dinner, seated in the best places, and given honor. We would never try to steal from our grandparents."

"That's the way it ought to be here," Mrs. Holland said. "And some people do treat their parents and grandparents with respect." She looked at Nicki. "I certainly hope Nicki will treat me with dignity when I'm older."

Nicki threw an arm around her mother's shoulder. "I'll give you and Dad the best room in my house."

Mrs. Holland chuckled. "I'm not sure that's what I'll want, but you girls need to be sure that a nursing home isn't the best thing for Mrs. Greaves. If she doesn't get better, if she can't care for herself, a nursing home might be what she needs. From the sale of her house and her furniture, she could afford a good place. Some of them are excellent facilities."

Mrs. Holland rifled through the papers on her desk and pulled out a glossy brochure. "Look at this place. I just helped a client and his wife find a home at the Pines Towers. These are really nice apartments for older people. They have nurses on staff to oversee any special medical needs people might have. But my client and his wife were really sold on it when they learned about the weekly concerts, trips, room-delivered meals, and games."

Nicki looked at the pictures of older people playing shuffleboard. "I don't know, Mom. Mrs. Greaves was lonely, but she had lived in that house for eighty years. I don't know if she could leave it."

"Well, we'll have to see what she wants to do when she gets better," Mrs. Holland said. "But her grandson may think he's doing the best thing for her."

Kim made a small snorting noise. It was so unlike her that everyone turned in her direction. "Mr. Simon wants to put his grandmother in Shady Grove—and that place is not excellent," Kim said. "I know."

Mrs. Holland closed her eyes and shook her head. "You're right, it isn't. Are you sure that's where the grandson wants her to go?"

Laura nodded. "We're sure."

Mrs. Holland opened her eyes and smiled at the girls. "Then do what you can to stop him."

Before the other girls left Nicki's house, Christine remembered the bundle of letters. She pulled them out of her purse. "Wait—what about these?"

Meredith looked at the faded ink. "Why don't each of us take a couple of them home and read them tonight? We can compare notes Monday morning."

"We also ought to find out what happened to Mrs. Greaves's furniture," Laura said. "What if Howard's planning a yard sale or something?"

Nicki nodded. "Okay, we'll check that out first thing after school on Monday."

But she frowned as she closed the door behind her departing friends. How would they find Mrs. Greaves's missing belongings? There wasn't a clue left in the house, and even if they had overlooked one, they couldn't go back without taking a chance on being arrested. Besides, they didn't have a key anymore.

Nicki had never felt more determined to stop Horrible Howard, but she'd also never felt less equipped.

—

Nicki couldn't sleep. She could hear the dull rumble of the television through the wall, so she knew her parents were still up. She got out of bed and tiptoed past her sleeping brother's and sister's rooms, then saw her parents sitting together on the sofa with a bowl of popcorn between them.

"Hey, Nicki." Her father saw her and grinned. "I thought the smell of popcorn might bring you out of hiding."

Nicki grinned, then pointed to a sight she'd never expected to see. "Look at that! Buttons and Stooge look like best buddies! When did that happen?"

Buttons lifted his head at the sound of his name, then gave Nicki a doggie grin and lowered his head back to the rug where he and Stooge were sleeping.

Mrs. Holland laughed. "Buttons must have figured that Stooge looked like a soft pillow. They've been lying there for hours."

Nicki's dad moved a pillow so she could sit down. "What's wrong, hon? Couldn't you sleep?"

Nicki plopped down next to her father and rested her head on his arm. "Dad . . . if you wanted to sell a lot of antiques and boxes of stuff, how would you do it?"

Her dad frowned. "Well, if it was just a few things, I'd have several antiques dealers come to the house and give me a bid. But if it was a lot, I'd hire an auctioneer and let him auction the stuff off. You can make a lot of money at an auction."

Nicki sat up straight and turned to face her parents. "An auction! That's it!"

"Are you thinking that's where Mrs. Greaves's furniture is?" her mom asked. "Her grandson couldn't sell anything without her permission . . . or unless he had power of attorney. That would be stealing."

Nicki folded her arms. "Mom, this man is a liar. Stealing would be nothing to him, especially if he thinks he won't get caught. And he won't if Mrs. Greaves doesn't get better and he moves her into Shady Grove."

"She won't get better in Shady Grove," her mother said. "It's a wonder the health department doesn't close that place down."

"We've got to help her get better, and fast," Nicki said, standing. "That means we have to find Peaches. We'll find her, stop the auction, and get Mrs. Greaves back into her house."

Mrs. Holland slapped the side of her head. "Why didn't I think of it before?"

"What?"

"John Phillips. Whenever we have to sell a house to settle the estate of someone who has died, we call John Phillips to clean out whatever's left inside. He handles estate auctions all over the state. Why don't you call him, Nicki?"

Nicki grinned. Now she had something to go on, a name that even sounded familiar. "I'll call him first thing Monday morning."

Her father reached out to pat her shoulder. "Think you can sleep now?"

"I'll try." Nicki grabbed a handful of popcorn and tossed a few kernels into her mouth. "But I still have a lot going on in my brain."

—

Nicki realized later in the night that her head wasn't busy; her stomach was. Some kind of virus had invaded, and she spent much of the night on her knees in the bathroom. She was sick, sick, sick. At three in the morning her mother checked on her, but there was nothing Mrs. Holland could do but say, "Call me if you need me."

"Thanks, Mom," Nicki muttered, "but I can be sick by myself."

As the sun rose, Nicki began to feel better. She crawled to her bed, knowing that her family would tiptoe past her room. She slept most of the morning, and when she woke later that afternoon, she found that everyone else in the family had left the house.

A note waited on the kitchen counter. "Nicki—we've cleared out so you can get the rest you need. Hope you're feeling better. Jell-O and chicken soup in the fridge if you feel like eating. XXOO, Mom."

Nicki didn't feel like eating, so she poured herself a tall glass of ginger ale. She sipped it slowly, waiting for memories of the long and awful night to recede so she could get back into the swing of things.

What could she do now? She didn't really feel strong enough to hop on her bike and go anywhere. She could call someone, but who? She wasn't quite in the mood for either Christine's goofy giggling or Meredith's intellectual discussions. Kim would sit in silent sympathy or offer wise sayings that only made sense half the time. Laura would want to talk about romance or shopping, and Nicki wasn't in the mood for either. So who did she want to talk to?

Scott, she realized, would be good to talk to now. They had always had a natural friendship—at least until she told him she couldn't go to the concert with him. But she couldn't and wouldn't call him now, especially since he had been flirting on purpose with Michelle and Corrin.

She looked at the phone. "I wish I could command you to ring," she said. "It's too quiet in this house. It's as quiet as Mrs. Greaves's house."

Something pricked her conscience at that moment and she realized that perhaps there were days—or maybe every day—when Mrs. Greaves had sat and asked the phone to ring.

Now it was Nicki's house that lay under a blanket of silence. She could hear the monotonous tick-tock of the clock in the hall and the fizz of the bubbles rising in her ginger ale. Something in the absolute loneliness was so awful that Nicki began to cry.

Fifteen

When Laura's driver dropped her off on Monday morning at the girls' usual before-school meeting place, Christine, Meredith, and Nicki were already waiting at the corner.

Christine set out with long steps. "Come on, Laura, we're in a hurry. We've got to meet Kim and make a phone call."

"Aren't we going to talk about what was in Lela's letters?" Laura asked, falling into step beside Nicki. "Mine didn't make much sense, but maybe when I put it together with the letters y'all had—"

"We'll do that in homeroom," Nicki said. "But right now we've got to meet Kim and make that call before the bell rings."

"Who are we calling?" Laura asked.

"John Phillips." Nicki pressed her hand to her side. She was walking so fast her ribs hurt.

"Who's John Phillips?" Laura asked, panting.

Nicki grinned. "You'll see. Now hurry up!"

—

Kim held Nicki's cell phone, her finger hovering above the send key.

"Are you sure you can imitate my mother?" Nicki asked again.

Kim drew a breath and said, "Welcome home, Nicki. Did you have a nice day?" She sounded so much like Mrs. Holland the other girls giggled.

Nicki grinned. "Okay, you can do it. Do you remember what to say?"

103

Kim nodded. "I think so."

Meredith tapped her watch. "Only three minutes until the bell. Better hurry."

Kim pressed the send key and held the phone to her ear. "I'd like to speak to John Phillips, please," she said in Mrs. Holland's voice.

When the man came on the line, Kim held the phone away from her ear so the others could hear, too.

"Mr. Phillips, I'm looking for a certain antique piece and I thought you might know where I could find one."

"Perhaps—what are you looking for?"

"An antique secretary," Kim said. "One with a glass door and a drop-down desk. Have you ever seen anything like that?"

The antiques dealer laughed. "You're in luck. There's an auction tomorrow night, a whole truckload of stuff from an old house, and I believe there's a very nice piece just like you described. I'll reserve it for you if you'd like to come by and take a look."

"The auction is tomorrow night?" Kim asked in her adult voice. "Where and what time?"

"The old Haynes ball field at seven o'clock, weather permitting. Come early if you want to take a look."

Meredith tapped her watch again, then silently mouthed "*Hurry.*"

"Thank you," Kim said. She disconnected the call just as the bell rang. "That was close," she said in her own voice as she handed the phone back to Nicki.

"But it worked." Nicki smiled as she dropped her phone into

her book bag. "And we know we have today and tomorrow to find Peaches."

—

After the homeroom announcements and Mrs. Balian's attendance check, the girls pulled out their letters from the bundle in the attic chimney. "My letters were to Lela from Alden," Christine whispered, "and apparently they were written during the time Lela was in school in Virginia."

The other girls nodded. "I think all our letters were from Alden," Nicki said.

Laura sighed. "I bet she hid them in the attic when she was engaged to Thomas Davis. She didn't want to throw them out, but she couldn't leave them lying around, either."

"Well, there's not much in my letters," Christine went on. "It's mostly general news about what was happening in town. I don't think Alden was much of a romantic. I get the feeling he and Lela were very good friends."

"In my letters Alden mentioned that Lela's father was ill," Meredith said, "but he said Lela shouldn't worry too much. He also mentioned that Eunice Brooke was visiting in Crystal Beach for the week."

"I remember reading something about Crystal Beach," Laura said, pulling out her letters. "Alden wrote that Eunice and Floyd went to Crystal Beach and that Lela's father was still quite ill."

Kim smoothed out her letters. "In the correspondence I read, Alden said that Peaches missed Lela very much."

Nicki ran her fingers over the faded ink on the pages in front of her. "My letters are mostly newsy notes. Alden did mention that Eunice was keeping company with Dan McBride. I think that means they were going together."

"Well, these were a real gold mine." Sarcasm dripped from Meredith's voice as she folded her pages and slipped them into her notebook. "We didn't learn a thing."

Christine's eyes began to glow. "Yes, we did."

Meredith frowned. "What'd we learn?"

"We learned that Alden Greaves was sort of a quiet childhood sweetheart," Laura said. "I bet he was the shy type."

"We learned that Eunice and her brother Floyd liked to vacation in Crystal Beach," Nicki said.

"We learned that Eunice had a boyfriend named Dan McBride," Laura added.

"And we learned that Mr. Huff was sick when Lela was away at school," Kim added. "She probably had to come home only when Mrs. Huff became too ill to care for him."

"Things were sure different in those days," Christine said. "Lela didn't stick her parents in Shady Grove so she could go out and party all the time."

Meredith shook her head. "Shady Grove didn't exist back then."

"Well, she still wouldn't have done it," Christian said. "She isn't the type. She's a nice person."

"What is the type?" Meredith asked. "I'm a nice person, but I couldn't handle being around old people all the time. Look at my mom—she's a grandmother, but she's in terrific shape. She's active, she's intelligent, and she's not going to get old. She's fighting old age with everything she's got."

Kim, who never got angry, leaned into Meredith's face and shook her finger. "Gray hair is a badge of honor," she said, her voice stern. "My father says it is earned by living well. It is an honor to be old and have gray hair."

"No way," Meredith snapped. "Being old may be better than being dead, but not by much."

Nicki crossed her arms, exasperated by her friends. "Can we have this discussion another time? We've got to find Peaches and we don't have much time."

"We don't have a lot to go on," Meredith said. "This may be a lost cause."

Laura lifted her hand. "We do have something. The Brooke family moved out of the house while Lela was away at school, right?"

Nicki made a face. "Maybe not exactly while she was away, but it was somewhere around then."

"Well, did you ever stop to think that maybe they moved to Crystal Beach? And maybe Eunice married her sweetheart Dan McBride. They were 'keeping company,' weren't they?"

Nicki grinned at her friend. "It's worth checking out. Crystal Beach is only twenty miles away. We could call directory assistance to see if there are any Brookes or McBrides listed in town."

"Before we do that," Meredith said, "I need a favor." She twisted in her chair. "My mom wants us to go with her to the spa again.

She's still too self-conscious to go by herself. Can we make our calls from the spa this afternoon? Mom said she'd take us to the hospital after her class if we still wanted to go visit Mrs. Greaves."

Kim, who was obviously still upset with Meredith's attitude, nodded stiffly.

"Okay," Nicki said. "We'll do our investigating from the spa. But if we come up empty-handed today, we'll be too late to stop the auction. If we can't stop the auction and save Mrs. Greaves's stuff, we might as well give up."

Sixteen

One of the counselors at the spa let the girls use a small cubicle to make their calls. As she dialed directory assistance, Nicki looked through the windows and saw waves of women bending, stretching, and jumping to the Tight and Trim counselor's chirpy orders.

"What city?" a mechanical voice asked.

"Crystal Beach."

"What name?"

"Floyd Brooke? Or Eunice Brooke?"

A moment of silence followed, then a human came on the line. "I have nothing under either of those names."

"How about Daniel McBride? Or Eunice McBride?"

The operator fell silent again, and Nicki braced herself for bad news.

"I have a D. B. McBride on Ocean View Lane."

"Really? I'll take it."

Another mechanical voice recited the number: 727-555-6920. Nicki scribbled the digits in her notebook.

Kim, Christine, Meredith, and Laura looked at the phone number. "That belongs to D. B. McBride," Nicki explained.

Meredith frowned. "That could be anybody. Daniel, Darlene, Dick, or even Delbert."

"But it's all we've got," Laura pointed out. "And I know that some women put their phone listing under their husband's names for security reasons."

"She's right," Nicki said. "Anyway, it wouldn't hurt to call and ask for Eunice. The worst that could happen is we'd get a wrong number."

The pumping music from outside the cubicle suddenly stopped as the exercise class finished. Mrs. Dixon wiped her face with a towel and stopped to talk with another woman.

"Should we wait to call?" Nicki asked, her hand on her cell phone. "Mrs. Dixon will be ready to leave in a minute."

"We could call from the hospital," Christine suggested. "Might be fun to call from Mrs. Greaves's room."

As they watched the ladies gathering towels and shoes, suddenly Mrs. Dixon's hand went to her mouth. She flushed, and for a moment Nicki thought she was having a stroke like Mrs. Greaves. But then Meredith's mother grabbed her towel, her keys, and ran toward the door.

Meredith had been watching, too. "Oh brother," she said, standing. "We'd better go. Something's upset Mom."

—

Mrs. Dixon sat with her head down and both hands on the steering wheel as the girls climbed into the SUV. Meredith sat next to her mother and whispered, "What's wrong, Mom?"

Mrs. Dixon swiped tears from her cheek and gave her daughter a wobbly smile. "It's really nothing—I feel stupid, really. But"—she choked on the words—"that woman asked me how many grandchildren I had!"

Nicki and Christine looked at each other. It was no secret

that Meredith's older brother and sister were both married and Meredith's sister had a baby.

Meredith patted her mother's back. "So? Didn't you tell her you had one grandson? What's wrong with that?"

"You—you don't understand," Mrs. Dixon said, reaching for a tissue. "I'm so embarrassed to do this in front of you girls, but someday you'll understand. I'm over forty, I don't have a husband, and I do have wrinkles and twenty extra pounds. If it weren't for the miracle of hair color, I'd have gray hair, too!"

Nicki thought of Shakespeare's Sonnet II. "Mrs. Dixon, you have so much! You're intelligent, you have students who appreciate you, and you have wonderful kids. You've accomplished a lot in forty years."

Meredith's mother groaned. "I'm sorry, Nicki, but I'm just not ready to age gracefully." She tossed the tissue onto the floor, then started the car. "Now, let me get you all to the hospital. While I'm there, maybe I ought to check myself in for a tune-up."

—

The girls gathered in a quiet corner and pulled out Nicki's cell phone for the third time that day. "Okay, who wants to call?" Nicki asked, offering the phone. "I'm too nervous."

Christine took the phone. "I'll do it. Just give me the number."

Nicki repeated the number, then held her breath as Christine dialed and put the phone to her ear.

"One ring," Christine said. "Two rings . . . three. I don't think anyone's home. Oh—hello?" Her eyes widened. "Oh, hello! My name is Christine Kelshaw and I'm a friend of Lela Greaves."

Nicki bit her lip and wished she could hear both sides of the conversation.

"Maybe someone in your family knew her as Lela Huff," Christine was saying. "I'm trying to find Eunice Brooke, and I thought she might be Mrs. Dan McBride."

Christine grinned and held up a finger, then pulled the phone away from her ear. Nicki and the other girls crowded closer as the crackly voice of an older woman came over the line: "Hello? You're looking for Eunice Brooke?"

Christine grinned and spoke louder. "I'm looking for Peaches Brooke."

The lady's laugh sounded like tinkling bells. "I haven't heard that name in years. I'm Peaches Brooke."

"You are?" Christine gripped the phone tighter. "Well, my friends and I know Lela Greaves—"

"Lela married Alden Greaves?"

"Didn't you know that?"

"No, I lost touch with Lela after she went back to school in— what was it? Back in '41?"

Christine smiled. "Close enough."

"Anyway, my family and I moved to Crystal Beach and my letters were returned from Virginia unopened. Later I heard her uncle had pledged her to marry Thomas Davis, and I knew he was planning to join the Davis clan in Pittsburgh. I thought she'd married him, gone up north, and forgotten all about me."

"She hasn't forgotten you," Christine said, pushing her bangs out of her eyes. "She's had a stroke and she keeps asking for you, over and over. The doctors think she'll get better a lot faster if she can see you."

"Oh my. Where is Lela?"

"Pine Grove Community Hospital."

"As close as that? You mean all this time, my old friend has been in Pine Grove?"

"She's been living in the same house," Christine said. "The same place she was born."

"You don't say! Why, this is wonderful news. I'll get my daughter to drive me up there tomorrow." The woman hesitated. "She really asked for me?"

"Yes, ma'am," Christine answered. "And it was nice talking to you. My friends and I are looking forward to meeting you tomorrow."

"Lands sakes. After all this time, to hear from Lela Huff."

The phone clicked and Christine handed it back to Nicki. "Peaches is coming tomorrow," she told the others, her eyes dancing. "Let's go tell Mrs. Greaves!"

—

The doctor was standing at the end of Mrs. Greaves's bed when Nicki and the girls peeked inside. "How is she today?" Nicki asked.

The doctor looked up and caught her eye. "She's sleeping now, but making progress. She had a good weekend and she's going home tomorrow."

"Home?" Christine snaked her way through the girls. "What home?"

"I believe her grandson has made all the arrangements," the doctor said, jotting a note on his chart. "You'll have to check with him."

"What's this?"

Nicki turned in time to see Howard Simon approaching. His eyes narrowed when he spied the girls talking to the doctor. "I thought I told you girls to stay away from my grandmother. You will only upset her."

Christine whirled on Howard like a determined lioness. "Where are you taking Mrs. Greaves? We know you're not taking her home to live with you."

Howard's face flushed, but he didn't waver. "She's going to a convalescent home," he said, slipping a hand into his pocket. "Everything's been arranged."

"Shady Grove is the pits!" Kim said.

"You can't sell her house," Nicki said, "and you can't auction her furniture without her permission."

Howard lifted his chin. "I can if the doctor signs a statement saying that Grandmother isn't able to make decisions for herself. As her grandson, I'm making decisions for her. I don't have to defend my actions to a group of nosy schoolgirls."

Nicki looked at the doctor. "Is that right?"

The doctor nodded and closed the cover on Mrs. Greaves's chart. "She may someday recover to the point of being able to care for herself, but at this point, that seems unlikely."

"I'm picking her up tomorrow," Howard told the doctor. "Just be sure she's ready to go."

Nicki and the others watched him go, then Nicki stepped closer to the doctor. "Sir, we've found the friend—Peaches—she wanted to see. There's a chance she will get better now, isn't there? Can't you keep her a few more days? Peaches is coming tomorrow."

Christine elbowed Nicki. "Look at that!"

Nicki followed Christine's pointing finger. Mrs. Greaves's eyes had opened, and her hand tugged at the blanket over her chest. "Peaches?" she asked, her words only slightly slurred.

Christine hurried to the old woman's bedside. "Yes, Peaches is coming. We found Eunice Brooke, and she's coming to see you tomorrow."

Nicki caught her breath when Mrs. Greaves chuckled. The doctor leaned closer. "Mrs. Greaves, would you let Peaches help you with your exercise?"

Mrs. Greaves smiled. "Ha, ha, the things we used to do," she said, her voice hoarse. "The fun we had. And to think that she's coming tomorrow . . ."

The doctor persisted. "Will you do your exercises now? I can have a nurse come in and show you how they're done."

Mrs. Greaves's brow wrinkled in a frown. "Young man, if my friend Eunice Brooke is coming tomorrow, I'll swim the breast stroke across the Gulf of Mexico!" She laughed again, a three-noted version of the old laugh that had been so full of life.

Nicki clapped and turned to the doctor. "Please?" she asked.

"Please keep her at least one more day?"

The doctor looked at Nicki, then studied Mrs. Greaves. "She was showing no significant signs of improvement until now," he said. "So I think the best thing would be to see how far she can go before we discharge her. And for that, I think we'll need at least two more days."

Seventeen

Meredith's mom waited in the parking lot until the girls came back from visiting Mrs. Greaves. "Guess what, Mom?" Meredith asked. "We found Peaches!"

"And she's coming tomorrow," Kim added, opening the car door.

"We beat Howard Greaves!" Christine said.

"For the moment, anyway," Nicki added.

"And if Mrs. Greaves gets better," Nicki said, "we can stop that auction tomorrow night!"

Mrs. Dixon waved her hands. "I'm confused."

Meredith climbed into the passenger's seat and was about to explain, but her mother shook her head. "Save it," she said, starting the car. "And you girls shouldn't get your hopes up. People don't recover from strokes overnight."

"She's already much better than she was," Nicki pointed out. "Every day we've seen a little progress. Now that we've found Peaches, I know she's going to get well fast. She just needed a little motivation."

"Well?" Meredith made a face. "She's old. She'll never be really well again."

"She can be well in her spirit," Kim said. "And that is most important."

Mrs. Dixon drove Laura out to her lovely home in Gatscomb Hills, then dropped Kim off at Levitt Park Apartments. Christine, Nicki, and Meredith's mom all lived near each other.

Mrs. Dixon had to drive right past Christine's house, so she dropped Chris off at the corner. Nicki laughed when she saw the Kelshaw home. As usual, the house literally bulged with the life of a large family. Music blared from an open window, a tricycle, two bikes, and a skateboard lay scattered over the driveway, and five pairs of muddy tennis shoes cluttered the sidewalk near the front door. No wonder Christine had enjoyed the peace and quiet of Mrs. Greaves's house!

"I'll call you in the morning to find out when we're going to the hospital," Christine called as she slammed the car door. "I can't wait to meet Peaches!"

"Sleep in for at least a while," Nicki reminded her. "Tomorrow's a holiday, remember?" School wouldn't start again until the Monday after Thanksgiving.

Mrs. Dixon smiled at the reminder. "Thanks, Nicki," she said. "Why don't you call your mom and ask if you can stay for supper? We're ordering pizza."

"That'd be great," Nicki said.

After checking with her mom, she and Meredith went into Meredith's room and collapsed on the twin beds.

Meredith sighed. "What a day."

"I know," Nicki said, "but I can't wait until tomorrow. I don't want to miss the big reunion of Peaches and Lela. I just hope Mrs. Greaves improves enough to stop the auction tomorrow night."

When Meredith didn't answer, Nicki propped herself up on one elbow and looked over at her friend. "What's wrong, Mere? I don't think you've enjoyed this investigation one bit."

Meredith sighed again, and Nicki thought she saw the glint of tears in the other girl's eyes. "It's just . . ." Meredith rolled onto her back and stared at the ceiling. "Being old seems such a waste. I mean, you spend your entire life learning things and doing things, but when you get old, you can't remember what you learned or do what you used to do. Old people can't use their brains anymore, and if I can't use my brain, I'll die. That's why I don't even want to think about getting old."

Nicki didn't know what to say, so she stayed quiet while Meredith drew a deep breath and kept talking. "Since the divorce, Mom has realized that she is starting over at the second half of her life. I mean, if the average lifespan in America is seventy years, my mom is already over halfway done. Can you imagine how that must feel?"

Nicki shook her head. "No. I feel like I have tons of years left."

"It's the pits," Meredith said. "And none of us knows how much time we have left."

"Girls!" Mrs. Dixon interrupted, calling up the stairs. "Pizza's here!"

Nicki and Meredith went into the kitchen, where two steaming hot pizzas waited in cardboard delivery boxes. Nicki knew it was an unwritten rule in both of Meredith's houses that no one sat down to eat unless they first picked up something to read.

Nicki found the habit annoying at first because she was used to conversation at mealtimes. But when she was at the Dixons', she pulled out a book and ate in silence like everyone else.

Mrs. Dixon put slices of pizza on three paper plates and picked up her newspaper. Meredith reached for a book at the end of the kitchen counter—*A Tale of Two Cities*. Nicki spied a *Reader's Digest* on the coffee table, so she made a quick detour into the family room and brought it to the kitchen table.

She skimmed through the humor sections and laughed at some of the stories. "I ought to send something in," she told Meredith. She pointed to the *Digest*. "They pay a lot of money for one of these little one-paragraph stories."

"Umm, that's nice," Meredith murmured, engrossed in her book.

Nicki took another bite of pizza and scanned the table of contents. The title of one article, "Disguised," caught her attention.

The story wasn't the mystery she'd hoped for. "Disguised," was the true story of a twenty-six-year-old woman named Pat Moore. Pat wanted to design products for elderly people, so in order to find out what they needed, she decided to become "old" herself.

Nicki read, fascinated, about how Pat Moore "aged" herself. An idea began to buzz in her brain.

"Meredith." She waited until *A Tale of Two Cities* dropped low enough for her to see her friend's face. "How would you like to help me perform an experiment tomorrow?"

"Like what?" Meredith asked.

Mrs. Dixon lifted a brow from behind her newspaper, but Meredith grinned. "I see that gleam in your eye, Nicki. What are you planning?"

"I want to surprise you," Nicki said. "Just don't plan anything for tomorrow morning and I'll be over early. Okay?"

Meredith nodded. "Okay. I'll be up, dressed, and ready for anything."

Eighteen

The next morning at eight o'clock, Nicki rang the Dixons' doorbell. Meredith answered, sleepy and still in her robe. "Can I change my mind?" she mumbled as she rubbed her eyes. "Somehow it seems wrong to be up this early during Thanksgiving vacation."

Nicki shook her head. "Just pretend it's an ordinary day."

Meredith stopped and sniffed. "What's that smell? Did you bring doughnuts?"

"My mom's homemade cinnamon rolls." Nicki lifted one of the bags so the aroma would reach Meredith's nose. "Now hurry up and let me in before they get cold."

When the girls had finished eating their breakfast, Nicki gave Meredith a sly smile. "I'm glad you haven't dressed yet." She pointed to her shopping bag. "I have your outfit in there."

"Outfit?" Meredith frowned. "Why do I need an outfit?"

Nicki pointed to the *Reader's Digest* on the table. "Pat Moore once disguised herself as an old person so she'd know what elderly people experienced," she explained. "I want to try the same experiment so we can know what life is like for someone like Mrs. Greaves."

Nicki knew anyone else would think this was a crazy idea, but the scientist in Meredith couldn't help but be interested. A flicker of doubt crossed Meredith's face for a moment, then she smiled. "Okay. What do we do?"

Nicki rummaged through her shopping bag. "First, old people can't hear so well, so I want you to put this soft wax in your ears.

122

It won't hurt you; it's the kind swimmers use to keep water out of their ear canals."

Meredith twirled the wax between her fingers for a moment, then put it in her ears. Mrs. Dixon wandered into the room and stared at the girls. "What are you two up to this early?"

"*What?*" Meredith asked, speaking too loudly. "I can't hear you."

Nicki looked at Meredith and nodded. The wax worked.

"Next," Nicki said, taking care to speak up, "old people often have cloudiness or cataracts in their eyes. If you put a couple of drops of baby oil in your eyes, your vision will be clouded."

Meredith slowly put her head back and allowed Nicki to drop baby oil into her eyes.

"Elderly people often have arthritis in their joints so they aren't flexible," Nicki said, "so I'm going to wrap your fingers and knees with ace bandages so you'll be stiffer. You can wear gloves and support hose so the bandages won't show."

As Nicki wrapped Meredith's fingers, elbows, and knees, she explained the project to Meredith's mother. Mrs. Dixon poured herself a cup of coffee, then sat down to sip it and watch her daughter's transformation.

"Finally," Nicki said, pulling a form-fitting foam ski vest from the bag, "if you wear this beneath your dress, it will make you look heavier and restrict your movements. You won't be able to bend easily at the waist."

"I hope you have a dress in that bag," Meredith said, taking the ski vest. "I don't have anything big enough to fit over all this stuff."

Nicki pulled a cotton housedress and a sweater from the bottom of her bag. "My grandmother's," she said. "She left them at our house the last time she visited. Also these." She pulled a pair of jogging shoes from the bag.

Meredith struggled to fasten the buttons of the housedress. "I need help," she said, wriggling her thick fingers. "I can't seem to get a grip on anything."

"She looks old," Mrs. Dixon said, studying her daughter over the rim of her coffee cup. "But what about her hair? We could pull it into a bun."

"And if you have baby powder, we could powder it," Nicki added.

"And that face." Mrs. Dixon smiled at Meredith's smooth complexion. "You need a few wrinkles, my dear. That twelve-year-old face isn't going to fool anyone."

Nicki looked at Meredith. Her friend had smooth, lovely black skin without even a trace of a wrinkle or a laugh line. "We'll pencil in some lines," she said, "but you should probably keep your head down as much as you can. Your teeth are too perfect, too, so keep your lips over your teeth if you can."

Nicki worked on Meredith's face with an eyebrow pencil while Mrs. Dixon powdered Meredith's hair. The ringing telephone interrupted them.

Meredith answered, then motioned to Nicki. "It's Christine.

She wants to know what time we're meeting at the hospital and how we are getting there?"

"Visiting hours don't begin until ten thirty," Nicki said. "Ask Chris if she and Laura can pick Kim up. You and I can meet them after we return from our experiment."

Meredith dropped her jaw. "You expect me to go somewhere like this?"

Nicki put the finishing stroke on Meredith's face, then stood back to survey her handiwork. "If you don't go anywhere, how will you learn anything? That's great—I think we're ready."

Meredith stood, slightly hunched over from the pressure of the tight ski vest. She looked like she had gained forty pounds. Her eyes were bleary and irritated from the eye drops, and from under her sweater, gloves covered her swollen fingers. Her hair was white and dull. With her face lowered, Nicki would almost believe she was looking at a seventy-year-old lady.

Until she walked. Meredith started for the door with strides that were much too athletic for an old woman. "Whoa," her mother called. "Where's the fire?"

"I like sneakers," Meredith said. "I like walking fast."

Mrs. Dixon held up a finger. "Hang on a minute. I have just the thing."

She returned a moment later with an elastic tube top. "Put this around your hips and thighs," she said, "and I guarantee you won't be able to take anything but little bitty steps."

Meredith complained, but the tube top worked. "Wow," she

said, inching her way across the kitchen, "this fabric is so springy I feel like I'm going to pitch forward at any minute."

"Okay, I think we're ready." Nicki pulled one last item from her bag. "Pretend that this straw purse has your Social Security check and everything you have to live on for the next month. Don't get distracted and leave it somewhere."

"Don't worry," Meredith said, taking the purse from Nicki. "I'm not brain-dead yet."

—

Nicki and Meredith were almost to the small convenience store near the entrance to their subdivision. They had only walked about half a mile, but Nicki took one step to every two of Meredith's and Nicki felt like she was sleep-walking compared to Meredith's labored trudging.

The day was gorgeous, with a warm sun and a cool breeze from the ocean, but Meredith worked up a sweat that even the November chill couldn't wipe away. "I don't know why I let you talk me into this," she muttered as they walked toward the store.

Nicki groaned. "I forgot about your voice! It's too young-sounding. Either croak a little or be quiet, or people will know you're only pretending."

As they crossed the street, a car pulled up to the stop sign and waited for the slow-moving girls to cross. The woman behind the wheel honked and yelled, "Milk it or move it, Grandma! I'm in a hurry!"

"How rude!" Meredith gritted her teeth. "I'm doing the best I can!"

When they finally reached the convenience store's parking lot, Nicki suggested that they enter separately. "Here's the experiment," she said. "Each of us will ask for directions, okay? We'll see if we're treated differently."

"Okay," Meredith said, still speaking louder than usual. "But I don't think this will prove anything."

Nicki breezed into the store and headed straight for the cashier. "Why, hello," the man behind the counter said. "What can I do for you today?"

"Can you tell me how to get to the hospital?" she asked. "At Main Street, do I turn right or left?"

The man smiled and stepped out from behind the counter. "Let me walk you to the window and I'll show you." He took her arm and pointed out the window. "Right there at that stoplight, you take a right. Go two blocks and you'll be in the hospital's parking lot. Anything else?"

Nicki thanked him with a smile. "I think I'll just stay here a minute and cool off. Thanks."

"Suit yourself." The man went back behind the counter and Nicki moved to the magazine racks. On every magazine cover, a young, wrinkle-free face smiled out at her.

Meredith came in then, hunched, sweaty, and obviously tired. She inched her way toward the cashier, her shoes squeaking across the tile floor.

The cashier didn't even look her way. "Excuse me?" Meredith whispered, her voice hoarse.

The man finally looked at her, but a shadow of irritation lay on his face. "Yes?"

"Can you give me directions to the, um, courthouse?"

The man sighed in exasperation. "Look, lady, I'm busy here. If you want directions, buy a map."

He turned his back to her, and Meredith turned slowly toward Nicki. In her friend's eyes, Nicki could see angry tears of frustration.

—

"That's it," Meredith said when they were outside. "I'm not taking another step in this getup. Okay, Nicki, you made your point. People are rude to old people—boy, are they rude! I'd give that guy a piece of my mind, but I have better manners."

Nicki reached out to soothe her upset friend. "Let's walk back to your place and get you out of that stuff."

"No way." Meredith collapsed on the sidewalk in front of the store. With her padded legs stretched stiffly in front of her, she looked like a tired old woman who sat down and couldn't get up again. "Call my mother, please, and see if she can come get us. I'm too pooped to walk home."

Nicki pulled her cell phone from her purse and dialed the Dixon apartment. The roars and rumbles of a group of motorcycles threatened to drown out her call, so she turned her back to them and covered her free ear.

Suddenly she remembered Meredith. She glanced over at her friend, who sat silent and still in front of a gang of leather-clad bikers.

One of the men walked up to Meredith and stood there. "Hey,

Grandma," he said. "Whatcha doin' here?"

Almost casually he reached for Meredith's straw handbag. "Come on, you know you ought to give it to me," he said.

Come on, Meredith, give it to him. It's only a straw purse.

For some crazy reason, Meredith hung on, then Nicki stared in horror when the man gave Meredith a swift kick in the ribs.

Meredith let out a healthy scream. The bikers ran away, laughing and scrambling. "That old lady's got a set of lungs on her!" one of them joked as he hopped on a Harley.

When they had pulled away, Nicki ran to Meredith's side. "Are you okay?"

Meredith wiped tears from her cheeks and nodded. "I'm okay," she said, but her voice trembled. "He didn't hurt me. How could he, with all this padding?"

Nicki looked at her friend. "Your mom's on her way. Are you sure you're okay?"

Meredith grasped Nicki's hand. "I'm okay," she said, "but I've got to tell you—I've never been so afraid in all my life."

"Did you see who they were? Would you recognize the guy who kicked you?"

Meredith shook her head. "Not with these cloudy eyes. They all looked alike to me."

"Hang on," Nicki said, helping her friend up. "Let's get you home and back to normal."

Nineteen

Mrs. Dixon was upset when she heard the story, and she took part of her frustration out on Meredith once the girls were safely in the car. "I'm taking you straight home so you can get out of that getup," she fussed. "If I had known this was going to be dangerous, I never would have agreed to this little experiment of yours."

"It's okay, Mom," Meredith said, calmer now. "I had the ski vest on, so I didn't feel a thing. And Nicki was there with me."

"But what if you hadn't had padding?" Mrs. Dixon fumed. "And what if it hadn't been an experiment? What if you'd been alone?"

"That's the point, Mrs. Dixon," Nicki said. "Real old people don't wear padding. And their life isn't an experiment. And most of them, like Mrs. Greaves, are alone."

Meredith looked at Nicki. "I never understood before how frightening getting old can be. I never thought of old people as, well, *people*. But today I realized that even though I looked, acted, and felt old, I was still *me*."

Mrs. Dixon reached out to pat her daughter's knee. "I guess I learned something from your experiment, too. Seeing you in disguise made me start thinking." She paused a moment as she turned into the driveway. "I guess getting old isn't so bad. There's a time for everything—a time for childhood, for mother-hood, even for being a grandmother. If I keep thinking I won't be happy unless I have a face-lift, a tummy tuck, and the body of a

130

twenty-year-old, well, I'll never be happy. And think of all the joy I'll miss."

"Well," Meredith said, struggling to grasp the door handle with her thick fingers, "I know I'll never be rude to another old person as long as I live."

Nicki leaned over and helped Meredith open the door. "Let's go wash your face and hair," she said. "There are people waiting for us at the hospital."

—

Meredith and Nicki found Christine waiting for them outside Mrs. Greaves's room. "It's simply wonderful," Christine said, her eyes bright. "I wish you could have been here when they first saw each other."

"I'm sorry we're late." Meredith was practically dancing now that her restrictive disguise was gone. "We performed an experiment. We'll tell you about it later."

Christine tapped Nicki's shoulder. "Before we go in, Nicki, I have a message for you."

"Oh yeah?"

Christine grinned. "Scott came by my house early this morning walking his dog. Or at least he said he was walking his dog. He asked where you were."

Nicki felt her face burn with a mixture of pleasure and embarrassment. "He did?"

Christine winked at Meredith. "When are you going to tell us about Scott?"

"There's nothing to tell." Nicki shrugged, but she was glad to hear Scott had asked about her. "We're friends, that's all. Now, let's go in, Chris—we're dying to meet Peaches."

Inside Mrs. Greaves's hospital room, Kim and Laura were sitting in chairs against the far wall. In the chair closest to Mrs. Greaves's bed was a plump little lady with golden cheeks and a big smile.

Nicki smiled at her. "You must be Peaches."

The lady beamed. "Nobody but my family and Lela ever called me by that name. My daddy said I had peaches in my cheeks, and the name stuck. Lela and I have been talking about those days all morning, haven't we, Lela?"

Mrs. Greaves said nothing, but she smiled up at Eunice McBride.

"We've also filled Mrs. McBride in on the situation with Howard," Laura told Nicki. "She's furious."

Mrs. Greaves patted her friend's hand and looked around the room. "It is so nice of you girls to come and visit for a spell," she said. "Do I know you?"

"She still doesn't remember the recent past," Christine whispered, "but she's talking up a storm and remembers everything about when they were growing up together. They've been having a ball."

Angry voices from the hall cut into the pleasant conversation. Meredith stepped back to peek into the hallway, then she shook her head. "Horrible Howard is back. He's out there arguing with the doctor."

An instant later the doctor stepped into the room, with Howard trailing in his wake. "I still say you can't keep her here,"

Howard said. "I'm going to have myself named as her legal guardian."

"I won't allow you to do that," the doctor said calmly, "because Mrs. Greaves has made such progress that she doesn't need a guardian. I will release her from the hospital when she's ready to go—and with whom she wants to go."

Mrs. Greaves looked up at Howard. "You remind me of my grandson," she said. "A fine boy, until his parents died. He could never accept that the accident wasn't his fault." She turned to Peaches and patted her hand. "That anger and guilt did something to him. He never cared about anything after that. Can you imagine? He wants to sell my grandpa's schoolhouse clock!"

Howard looked away as his face flooded with color. Mrs. McBride gave him a stern look. "Don't you know that you've broken your grandmother's heart? I understand from these girls that you've made some arrangements concerning Lela's house and her belongings. Is that true?"

Howard didn't answer.

"Well," Mrs. McBride went on, "I want you to know that my son is a judge. If you touch or sell one item of property belonging to this woman, I will call the proper authorities. So if there's someone you should call, young man, I suggest you do it now."

Eunice Brooke McBride raised her chin and didn't blink as she finished. "If you can't appreciate Lela Greaves, then you have no business handling her affairs. We will find someone else."

As Howard turned on his heel and left the room, Mrs. McBride turned to Christine. "Did I say that right?" she asked, smiling. "I'll bet he's calling that auction fellow right now to cancel the sale."

Mrs. McBride then turned to Mrs. Greaves and took her hand. "Lela, I'm living in Crystal Beach with my daughter. We have a lovely old house near the ocean and no one to share it with. Why don't you move in with us? You can bring whatever you like from your place. It'll be just like old times."

Mrs. Greaves smiled as if the idea delighted her. "The ocean? I've lived on the river so long, the beach might be a nice change. I'd love to come."

Mrs. McBride nodded. "Then you must do your exercises so you can regain your strength. We'll have you walking up and down the beach in no time."

Mrs. Greaves nodded, then she looked at the doctor. "Let's get busy, young man," she said. "I want to go home. My friend and I have an appointment to walk on the beach."

The doctor smiled. "Hold on, Mrs. Greaves. You know we can't turn back time. You will have to deal with the effects of this stroke for a while."

"I didn't ask you to make me young again," Mrs. Greaves answered. "All I want is to keep on getting older." She smiled at the girls. "Growing old is wonderful if you have a friend along for the ride."

Mrs. McBride nodded at Nicki. "I want you girls to know that you can visit us any time. I'm sure Lela will want Buttons brought home if you can bear to part with him."

"Oh sure," Nicki said, thinking of Stooge's patience with the lively visitor. "I already have a dog. We'll all come to visit when we bring Buttons to your house."

The girls stood to leave. Mrs. McBride gave each of them a hug and a smacky kiss on the cheek.

"I know Lela doesn't remember everything," she said, holding Nicki's shoulders, "but I understand and appreciate all you've done. This year's Thanksgiving will be extra special."

Meredith blinked her eyes. "Every year is special, isn't it?"

As they filed out the door, Nicki heard Mrs. Greaves ask Peaches: "What nice girls they are. Are they friends of yours?"

"Absolutely," Mrs. McBride answered. "They are friends of ours."

The Case of the Teenage Terminator

Tommy's troubles could mean danger for
Nicki and her friends!

With a burst of nervous energy, Nicki dove to the safety of the windowless side of the shed. As the others glided into place beside her, she put her finger across her lips and knelt to listen.
"It's too hot in here," a voice said.
"It's too hot everywhere tonight, after your brilliant move," another voice answered. "I hope you're not planning on hiding out here until everyone calms down. You'll be here a week."

Christine's brother Tommy is in trouble, but he doesn't seem to realize it. Nicki, Meredith, Christine, Kim, and Laura take on an investigation that pits them against a danger they've never faced before—one that could lead to a life-or-death struggle.

About the Author

Angela Hunt lives in Florida with her husband Gary, their two children, and two mastiffs (really big dogs). Her favorite color is periwinkle blue and she loves pizza. You can read more about her, her dogs, and her books at www.angelahuntbooks.com.